Essentials for Blended Learning

W9-DCX-102

Essentials for Blended Learning: A Standards-Based Guide provides a practical, streamlined approach for creating effective learning experiences by blending online activities and the best of face-to-face teaching.

This guide is:

- Easy to use: Clear, jargon-free writing; illustrations; and references to online resources help readers understand concepts.
- Streamlined: A simple but effective design process focuses on creating manageable activities for the right environment.
- Practical: Real-world examples from different subject areas help teachers understand principles in context.
- Contemporary: The variety of modern, connected technologies covered in the guide addresses a range of teaching challenges.
- Forward-looking: The approach bridges the gap between formal classroom learning and informal lifelong learning.
- Standards-based: Guidelines and standards are based on current research in the field, relevant learning theories, and practitioner experiences.

Effective blended learning requires significant rethinking of teaching practices and a fundamental redesign of course structure. *Essentials for Blended Learning: A Standards-Based Guide* simplifies these difficult challenges without neglecting important opportunities to transform teaching. This guide is suitable for teachers in any content area.

Additional content is available at essentialsforblended.com

Jared Stein is Director of Knowledge Resources at Instructure.

Charles R. Graham is a Professor of Instructional Psychology & Technology at Brigham Young University. He also currently serves as the Associate Dean for the David O. McKay School of Education.

Essentials of Online Learning Series

Series Editor: Marjorie Vai

Essentials of Online Course Design: A Standards-Based Guide
Marjorie Vai and Kristen Sosulski

Essentials for Blended Learning: A Standards-Based Guide
Jared Stein and Charles R. Graham

Essentials for Blended Learning
A Standards-Based Guide

Jared Stein and
Charles R. Graham

Routledge
Taylor & Francis Group

NEW YORK AND LONDON

First published 2014
by Routledge
711 Third Avenue, New York, NY 10017

and by Routledge
2 Park Square, Milton Park, Abingdon, Oxon OX14 4RN

Routledge is an imprint of the Taylor & Francis Group, an informa business

Typeset in Helvetica Neue and Optima
by Florence Production Ltd

Library of Congress Cataloguing in Publication Data
Stein, Jared.
  Essentials for blended learning :a standards-based guide/
  by Jared Stein and Charles Graham.
  pages cm.
  Includes bibliographical references and index.
  1. Blended learning. 2. Computer-assisted instruction. 3. Educational technology—Standards. I. Title.
  LB1028.5.S715 2014
  371.3—dc23
  2013009882

ISBN: 978-0-415-63615-5 (hbk)
ISBN: 978-0-415-63616-2 (pbk)
ISBN: 978-0-203-07525-8 (ebk)

Contents

Contents

Foreword

Having taught both in classrooms and online for over twenty years, I am sometimes amazed at what is considered new and innovative. Even before the World Wide Web revolutionized our approach to distance education, many were experimenting with using various technologies to extend and enhance classroom instruction and take learning beyond the classroom walls. As technologies developed, networks grew, and our practices matured and evolved. Together, we developed an approach to teaching and learning that is now more often blended than not, using a multitude of tools and techniques to support human learning and development. As Charles Graham described in the opening chapter to *The Handbook of Blended Learning* almost a decade ago, mixing delivery and interaction modes in education has been going on for a long time. Yet very few practical resources exist for the teacher who wants to strategically redesign a course into a blended experience for her students.

As I read through this book, I am already thinking of the colleagues, teachers, instructional designers, and graduate students who I know will find this extremely valuable. As a practical guide to designing and teaching a blended course, I personally haven't read anything more useful. Since more and more courses in higher education today use some form of blended instruction—even just haphazardly—it is critical that we provide approachable guidance to instructors and the designers who support them.

One of the great challenges in writing a book like this is the **need to incorporate best practices for both online and face-to-face environments**, and then to guide readers as they choose combinations of each mode that will lead to effective, engaging, and efficient learning environments. That's hard enough to do well as an individual designer or instructor, and the effective way that the authors have found to support the efforts of others is a testament to their expertise—both in the field of blended learning and as teachers, basically just helping others learn. The bulk of this book (Chapters 4–8) provides specific, practical design guidance. When the exact form of the intended outcome, in this case a unique blended learning design and course, is often impossible to prescribe, the challenge of providing design guidance that is effective time and time again is real and substantial.

This book doesn't just provide design guidance, but it also explains the **fundamental values and benefits that blended learning offers** learners, teachers, and institutions. It is important for teachers (and administrators) to appreciate the potential benefits and acknowledge the challenges of adopting blended learning practices.

Having the fundamental principles and a description of best practices that support blended learning provides a solid sense of knowledge, but teachers and designers also need to develop skill in blended course design. A step-by-step, iterative design process may be the easiest and yet most thorough way of approaching that skill development. Principles of rapid prototyping resonate with many teachers who develop and revise their own courses already, and a deliberate and reflective approach to this practice can boost the quality and speed with which quality blended courses are produced.

Just as viewing detailed descriptions of others' blended designs offers teachers insights and ideas that can lead to continual improvement, so can reflecting on their own course designs, teaching, and experiences—both as a learner and as a teacher. Reflective practices such as this are likely to stimulate innovative thinking as the reader combines personal experiences from the past, current practices used today, and new approaches encountered in the text into a unique blend that fits his students, his content, and himself as teacher.

As the shape of blended learning (and, indeed, all of education) continues to change and evolve over the coming years, essential elements of effective, engaging, and efficient design will remain. I expect this book to continue to be a valued resource for teachers as long as we are using technologies to bridge gaps among learners, teachers, ideas, and content. That, I propose, will never change.

Brian J. Beatty
Associate Vice President for Academic Affairs Operations
San Francisco State University
San Francisco, CA
April 2013

Introduction to this Guide

This is the second in the Routledge series on Essentials of Online Learning. The first book, *Essentials of Online Course Design: A Standards-Based Guide*, walked you through the process of creating a purely online course. While many of the principles in that book apply to the online portions of a blended course, the overall approach in developing a course that is partly online and partly onsite is quite different because it requires:

- recognition of the relative strengths and weaknesses of each mode;
- a design strategy that focuses on learning outcomes, not technology;
- interweaving of activities between modes to diminish "distance" and engage students in a developing community.

This book features examples from blended courses that show how onsite and online experiences can be most effectively utilized. Additionally, specific blended design and teaching strategies leverage differences between traditional, face-to-face, and online environments.

i.1 A Unique Guide to Designing Blended Learning

This guide aims to provide teachers and designers with a practical, standards-based approach to developing effective learning experiences that blend relevant online technology and the best of face-to-face learning. This guide is:

- **Standards-based.** Guidelines and standards are based on current research in the field, relevant learning theories, and practitioner experiences. Standards checklists enable readers to reflect and self-evaluate their work.

- **Easy to use.** The book's design combines text, illustrations, and references to online resources to help readers make sense of concepts. The writing is concise and clear, and avoids jargon.
- **Streamlined.** The guide utilizes a simple but effective design process that focuses on manageable activities for the right environment.
- **Practical.** The book uses real-world examples from different subject areas to help teachers understand principles in context. While it is grounded in theory, it is not about theory. The book also provides tips, notes, and opportunities to pause and think through ideas.
- **Expansive.** Each chapter includes references for further reading, and a companion website opens even more doors.
- **Contemporary.** The book recognizes the increasing variety and power of modern, connected technologies that address a variety of teaching challenges.
- **Forward-looking.** Bridging the gap between formal, classroom learning and informal, lifelong learning is both a challenge and an opportunity in the modern world. This book presents ideas that encourage authentic learning experiences and extends beyond the limitations of the traditional classroom.

i.2   Who is the Guide For?

This guide is for those involved with blended teaching and training at all levels, including:

- **Teachers** challenged with redesigning a face-to-face or online course into a blended mode.

- **Instructional designers and technologists** working with teachers to apply models, examples, and principles of the blended course through a standards-based approach.

- **Staff development trainers** who may use this guide as a framework or primary resource for a staff development program on blended teaching.

- **Instructors** teaching courses on blended learning design in schools of education, who may use this guide to reduce the burden of developing resources of their own.

- **Students** in educational technology programs exploring blended learning in their studies or internship experiences.

- **Administrators** who want to learn more about blended teaching, or who may even be skeptical about the effectiveness and practicality of online or blended courses.

i.3 A Standards-Based Approach

It is increasingly important that educators recognize the impact of technology on the way we live our lives, and on how their students will interact in the world after school. Teachers shouldn't employ technology just for technology's sake, but to improve learning outcomes and increase learner engagement. Administrators and managers must ensure that new teaching approaches meet or exceed learning expectations. This guide's standards-based approach addresses those needs without overwhelming teachers with theory.

Many standards that are applicable to online course design are similarly applicable to blended course design. Indeed, many of the standards set out elsewhere in this series are broadly applicable to education and learning design in general.

However, because blended courses have fundamental differences, we introduce new standards to serve what we see as the critical needs of blended course design.

Essentials for Blended Learning: A Standards-Based Guide employs a step-by-step approach to creating a blended course. The standards are woven into the content of each chapter, and reinforced throughout the book in ways that facilitate reflection and self-evaluation as teachers work through the blended course design process.

We present standards in three stages:

1. *Within each chapter, as they are covered.* At this stage, they look like this:

    ☑ Resources and activities support learning outcomes.

2. *At the end of each chapter, in the summary* to facilitate review or as a focused checklist. At this stage, they look like this:

    ☐ Resources and activities support learning outcomes.

3. *As a complete checklist in the appendices* to guide and evaluate your blended course design. At this stage, they look like this:

    ☐ Resources and activities support learning outcomes.

The redundancy built into this small guide reinforces your understanding of the essentials of good blended course design, and should help you to recognize the sometimes subtle interconnectedness of the standards.

Underlying Principles

These standards have been culled from a number of resources—most of which are included as references at the end of the chapters in which they most prominently appear. These standards come from published research results, educational theories, or "best practices" in blended teaching and learning. Some of the standards are born of the authors' own experiences designing and teaching blended courses and training teachers to design and teach their own blended courses.

i.4 Organization of the Book

The book is organized to introduce and guide you to a blended course design process:

- **Chapter 1: Orientation to Blended Teaching and Learning** explains how blended learning not only provides great flexibility and opportunity for enhancing learning with technology, but also speaks directly to phenomena we are experiencing in our increasingly technology-imbued lives.

- **Chapter 2: Elements of Blended Courses: A Tour** walks you through several examples of blended course design, focusing on overall approaches, specific activities, and technology used.

- **Chapter 3: Engaging Learners in a Blended Course** precedes the actual blended course design process by exploring the opportunities for and advantages of purposefully engaging learners by addressing both the mind and the heart.

- **Chapter 4: Designing Blended Courses** prompts teachers to rethink their course in anticipation of a blended redesign. This chapter introduces an easy-to-follow design process that aims to ensure your choice of modes is best for learning.

- **Chapter 5: Planning Your Course from Goals and Outcomes** helps teachers set a solid foundation for a learning-centered blended course. High-level course goals are supported by specific learning outcomes that lead to blended assessments and activities.

- **Chapter 6: Blending Assessment and Feedback for Learning** focuses on the importance of feedback in assessments and the advantages that blended courses offer by enabling a mix of online and onsite assessment methods.

- **Chapter 7: Blending Content-Driven Learning Activities** and **Chapter 8: Blending Community-Driven Learning Activities** explain and illustrate how to design and create learning activities that enhance flexibility, effectiveness, and engagement, whether online or onsite. This chapter emphasizes learning activities that are backed by research in both modes.

- **Chapter 9: Weaving it All Together** focuses on the deliberate interweaving of onsite and online activities as teachers build the course's lesson patterns, home page, and syllabus.

- **Chapter 10: Ongoing Improvements of the Blended Course** prompts teachers to reflect on and evaluate their blended teaching practices using various tools and strategies, and to continue to improve their blended course design.

Appendices are provided for your reference, including: Blended Course Standards Checklist and Key Cognitive Processes in Bloom's Taxonomy.

i.5 How to Use the Guide

This guide is intended to be used **while designing a blended course**. We recommend that you read everything and examine each example as you work through the course design process. However, depending on your time frame and what you already know, you may find that you are best served by jumping into a specific topic directly.

After you gain an understanding of blended learning through examples of blended course designs in Chapters 1–3, you'll be prepared to dive into the blended course design process that we explain in Chapter 4. Take the time to read through these chapters if you want a deep understanding of what's possible with blended learning, and how that influenced the content of this guide.

Chapters 5–9 are the core functional chapters of blended course design, and can be used as a step-by-step process that takes you from course goals to a single lesson prototype and beyond to the development of a blended course website.

Start here if you are already familiar with blended courses and instructional design processes, or if you are beginning another blended course design.

Key sections of the book invite you to enhance your reading experience online by visiting essentialsforblended.com.

i.6   Terminology in this Guide

For the sake of consistency and simplicity, we have used specific words or phrases to represent, in some cases, a variety of possibilities:

- **Teacher.** The course designer/developer, instructor, professor, facilitator, or trainer. In cases where the distinction between teacher/instructor or designer/ developer is important, the context will make that clear.

- **Student.** The individual who is taking the online course (i.e. the trainee, class member, or participant).

- **Learner.** This term is used when we refer to a student beyond a course, with respect to the ways people develop knowledge.

- **Course.** We use this term for the structured set of goals and outcomes as designated by the teacher or institution. "Course" covers any of the following: university or college course, high school course or class, training program, seminar, or workshop.

- **Class.** The community of teacher(s) and students organized around common goals of learning. Whereas "course" refers to the structure of content, assessments, and activities, "class" refers to the people engaged in the course.

- **Lesson.** Sometimes referred to as modules, units, lectures, chapters, or sections, a lesson is a cohesive unit of instruction organized around specific learning outcomes, and containing learning activities and assessments.

Lessons are the building block of any course. In a blended course, lessons contain activities that happen online as well as onsite.

- **Goal.** Sometimes called a course-level outcome or objective, we use "goal" to refer to learning objectives that are broad, harder to measure, and encompass several specific learning outcomes.

- **Outcome.** A specific, measurable statement of desired learning—whether knowledge, behavior, attitude, etc.—upon successful completion of a learning experience.

- **Learning Management System (LMS).** A Web-based system of tightly integrated tools and technologies constructed to help teachers manage instruction, facilitate activities, and monitor learning. It is a commonly used virtual environment where learners engage with content and the class community. An LMS is sometimes called a Course Management System (CMS) or a Virtual Learning Environment (VLE).

- **Onsite.** Meeting or activities happening face-to-face, in the traditional classroom setting.

- **Online.** Synchronous (real-time) or asynchronous activities happening on the World Wide Web or via Internet technologies.

- **Gender.** We arbitrarily use either male or female genders in examples throughout our writing.

Chapter 1

Orientation to Blended Teaching and Learning

Immediate access to people and information through technology is increasing, and this is transforming our everyday lives. Using connected mobile tools such as smartphones, tablets, and laptops, we purposefully "blend" physical and online activities to create optimal experiences. This is what blended education is all about: situating learning experiences online or onsite based on the relative strengths and weaknesses of each mode.

Blended courses provide the opportunity for teachers to mix the best of onsite and online to create a new learning environment for their students. Research suggests that blended courses can have a positive impact on efficiency, convenience, and learning outcomes. By moving more of the learning to online environments, blended courses add flexibility to participants' schedules, provide learning benefit through automated and asynchronous online tools, and can tap into the modern, social Web to help learners venture beyond the traditional confines of the classroom.

To consistently achieve such benefits, teachers need to go beyond a simple "digital facelift." Instead, teachers should aim to create transformative blends through an intentional course redesign process.

1.1 Changing World, Changing Learners

David Wiley, Professor of Instructional Psychology and Technology at Brigham Young University, describes six significant changes in our everyday lives brought on by the growth of technology, especially Internet technology (Wiley 2006). Wiley suggests we are moving from:

- **Analog to digital.** Information, media, interactions, and experiences are increasingly done online.

- **Tethered to mobile.** Wireless networks, laptops, smartphones, and tablets allow people to access the digital world anywhere, anytime.
- **Isolated to connected.** On the Web, we can connect to people around the world, however we want. Niche interest groups thrive, professional connections grow exponentially, and we never have to lose touch with family and friends.
- **Generic to personal.** No longer do we have to be satisfied with one view of news, one stream of information, or one type of community. Individuals can choose their own experiences, and can have that delivered to their personal devices.

A Day in the Connected Life

Devlin uses his smartphone to start his day by checking his task list and calendar while eating breakfast. On his bus ride to work, his phone notifies him that his teacher has posted a new grade and given feedback on Devlin's latest blog post. Devlin quickly reads the feedback through a mobile app, and begins thinking about revisions he might make.

At work, Devlin quickly searches the Web for information to support an urgent project that his team has just been assigned. He quickly compiles the information into an online document, and adds his teammates as coauthors so they can collaborate digitally and share their plans with the entire company.

At lunchtime, Devlin reaches out to a friend in another department via text message, and they both use online social media services to get recommendations for a local restaurant. The restaurant turns out to be pretty good, and Devlin rates it on his favorite social network site so his friends and family can learn about it.

After work, Devlin loads his university's Learning Management System (LMS) on his tablet and watches a video explanation recorded by his teacher. This leads him into an online discussion forum, where he reads through many of his classmates' posts before his bus stop. He now has a head start on his course responsibilities, and will process what he's seen and read while he does some household chores.

Thanks to nearly constant access to the Internet, Devlin's daily life is blended with online services and information that allows him to accomplish more, efficiently and spontaneously.

- **Consuming to creating.** The modern Web makes creating and participating as easy as consuming—and vastly more fulfilling. The changes from analog to digital and tethered to mobile are reflected in our steadily increasing access to connected technology, and signal the others in this list. YouTube and Flickr exemplify social media by providing a space for everyone to share their own videos and photography. Blogs provide individuals with their own spaces for linked writing and showcasing of their work. Wikipedia is history's largest encyclopedia, crowdsourced by volunteer experts and amateurs from around the world.

- **Closed to open.** For better or for worse, citizens of the Web are increasingly open about who they are and what they do. This helps people find and develop connections and communities. Open sharing on the Web is also becoming the norm, where individuals recognize the value of contributing their efforts to the global network of information and ideas.

How well has education kept up with these changes? Some schools may have adapted to the first two or three by providing online education. But even then, many teachers tend to simply transfer what they've always done in the onsite classroom to the online environment. This kind of "digital facelift," as Gardner Campbell puts it (Campbell & Groom 2009), is insufficient to realize our learners' potential in the twenty-first century.

Learners growing up in our current technology-imbued environment are sometimes referred to as "digital natives." Mark Prensky first defined digital natives as the incoming generations of learners who are not only broadly skilled in the use of new technology, but also fully expectant that technology will be available in all aspects of their lives—anytime, everywhere (Prensky 2001). While this classification of learners' ability by generation has been the target of some criticism, it has drawn attention to an important and fundamental shift in learners' expectations. Susan Metros suggests that the one thing we *can* say about today's learners is that they'll go to the Web before the textbook or teacher (Metros 2011).

This is probably a good thing. The wealth and availability of information continues to grow at astounding rates, and the skills and knowledge that workers need to thrive in this twenty-first century are ever changing. Allan Collins and Richard Halverson argue that we are moving from an era of "universal schooling" to an era of "lifelong learning," learning continually, as new situations demand (Collins and Halverson 2009). To be effective, learning will be just-in-time, geared to the learner's particular and immediate needs. Most of the learning that happens in people's lives will not happen in the classroom, but in the workplace and via social connections. Jay Cross of the Internet Time Alliance suggests that informal learning is not the exception, but the norm: as much as 80 percent of our learning happens outside the classroom (Cross 2006).

We need to respond to this changing world by teaching and learning *differently*.

1.2 What is Blended Learning?

Though there is no single definition of "blended," this guide focuses on blended courses as a combination of onsite (i.e. face-to-face) with online experiences to produce effective, efficient, and flexible learning.

If one imagines a spectrum of technology enhancement, with traditional onsite on the left and fully online on the right (Figure 1.1), a blended course could fall anywhere in between the two. Some institutions designate a certain percentage of the traditional onsite meetings be replaced with online activities, but these designations are generally arbitrary.

And they depend on your perspective: an online course becomes blended as soon as it introduces onsite, face-to-face meetings. Typically, an onsite course becomes blended when online activities are designed to *replace* onsite sessions.

Reducing the number of onsite meetings is one way that blended courses move beyond simply technology-enhanced or Web-enhanced courses. A three-credit course that meets on

Tip
Avoid the "course and a half" syndrome, where a blended course becomes more work simply by adding to—not replacing—onsite activities. Chapter 4 addresses this challenge.

onsite   blended   online

Figure 1.1 A spectrum of technology-enhanced teaching or learning

Tuesdays and Thursdays might, as a blended course, meet only on Tuesdays (Figure 1.2). In the space of the week, students may watch an online video, discover additional resources, engage in an instructor-led online discussion with their classmates, take an online quiz, or review peers' draft papers.

Another blended course design may have the class meet onsite just a few times throughout the semester. For example, a blended course may meet once at the beginning, and once at or just before the end of the semester. This sets the onsite sessions as a frame for the online experiences, which constitute the majority of the course.

This guide focuses on the former blended model, where onsite and online experiences are interwoven throughout the term or semester. The latter model is still a blended model, but its design process is more closely aligned with fully online courses (see Vai & Sosulski 2011).

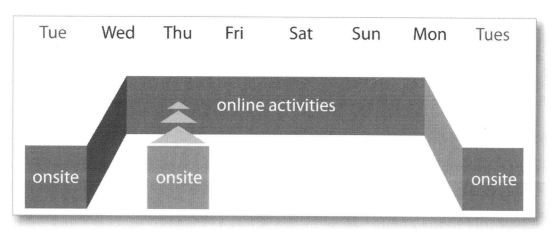

Figure 1.2 Moving learning experiences online

Blending is more than just replicating onsite activities in online environments. We think the aim of any effort toward blending should be transformative, resulting in better learning than previous modes of delivery.

1.3 Why Blend?

We suggested that many people live their lives "blended," as a mix of physical and online activities and experiences. Blended learning not only fits into the modern, connected lifestyle, but can also provide specific benefits to students, teachers, and administration:

- increased access and convenience;
- improved learning;
- decreased (or more flexible) costs.

All of these benefits can be obtained if blended course design is done intentionally, with a purposeful course design process and adherence to standards.

Hybrid versus Blended—The term "hybrid" is often used interchangeably with "blended," though blended is the more commonly used of the two.

Increased Access and Convenience

When done right, blended courses allow for increased access and convenience without giving up—and sometimes even enhancing—the things that many students associate with a satisfying, effective learning experience (for instance, building relationships with teachers and classmates).

The value of online courses for many students is that they no longer have to come to campus to take the course. For nontraditional students, who may work or have a family to care for, online courses can mean the difference between achieving goals and stagnating in a dead-end career. While still requiring some onsite attendance, blended courses provide more flexibility and freedom than purely onsite courses by moving a significant amount of onsite class sessions online.

The simple use of technology to facilitate learning activities provides added flexibility, because now students and teachers can participate in the course when most convenient.

The "hyflex" model of blended courses provides students with the option of coming to onsite sessions if and when they choose (Beatty 2010). This requires that teachers create a fully online course with *optional* onsite components that can substitute for online activities. This model is more intensive to create, but offers maximum flexibility and the power for individual students to choose what's best for them.

Smartphones and tablets can support online interactions during commutes on public transportation or whenever users have spare time, using the tools they already have.

Improved Learning

Educational research suggests blended courses are more effective compared to both face-to-face and online. A 2009 US Department of Education report examined fifty-one empirical studies comparing online education with traditional face-to-face courses and concluded, "students who took all or part of their class online performed better, on average, than those taking the same course ... face-to-face" (Yates et al. 2009, p. xiv).

The report also compared blended courses with fully online courses and found that "instruction combining online and face-to-face elements had a larger advantage ... than did purely online instruction" (p. xv).

Why is blended as effective or even more effective than onsite courses? There are no complete answers, but some ideas include:

- **Improved instructional design.** Blended courses (like online courses) may be more intentionally designed than face-to-face counterparts, if only because institutional initiatives for blended courses often involve instructional designers or educational technologists who support the faculty in a scheduled redesign process.

- **Increased guidance and triggers.** Students working in a face-to-face class receive guidance from the teacher during class time and from a syllabus when working on their own. In a blended course, the course environment provides a clear path through resources, activities, and assessments with explicit guidance each step of the way.

● **Easier access to learning activities.** Putting materials and activities online allows more of the class to engage with these on their own schedule, which may lead to more complete learning.

● **Individualized learning opportunities.** Because digital materials may be accessed according to students' individual needs, and reviewed upon demand, the provision of digital materials allows students to self-direct certain learning activities to fill their knowledge gaps. Automated assessments often used in online learning environments may also provide immediate, corrective feedback that directs students to revisit materials.

● **Increased engagement through social interaction.** Students in a face-to-face course may have limited opportunities to engage with each and every one of their classmates, and the face-to-face environment itself may inhibit some students from participating. Online environments that facilitate class discussions, collaboration, etc. may increase the amount of student-to-student interaction. This may, in turn, enhance their engagement with the subject matter and provide motivational benefits from the increased social interaction.

● **Time on task.** Blended and online courses tend to intensify student focus on more relevant work through the course website. This may be true because of increased guidance and access, and improved instructional design as described above. It may also be that time on task is simply more visible in a blended course because student activity in an online environment can be tracked on every page and every click.

Decreased (or More Flexible) Costs

Blended courses can decrease costs to teachers, students, and institutions. Teacher and students can benefit from less travel time, transportation savings, and fewer parking costs.

From an institutional perspective, use of physical campus resources can be reduced. When a blended course cuts its onsite time by at least 50 percent, this reduction can provide significant resource savings to institutions challenged with maximizing physical classroom space. Using the example of a Tuesday/Thursday class referenced above (Figure 1.2), we can see that this opens the Thursday classroom slot for another blended course, essentially doubling the classroom's scheduling capacity (Figure 1.3).

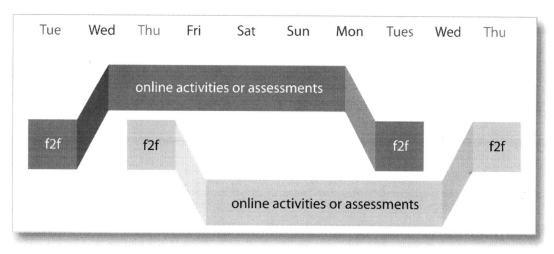

Figure 1.3 Two blended courses maximizing a single classroom

Trending toward Blending

As technology has advanced, we've seen more and more "traditional" courses adopt technology. This usually starts small, by posting a syllabus online, communicating via email, or posting slides or lecture notes. This has allowed traditional courses to take advantage of technology efficiencies without forcing faculty out of their pedagogical comfort zone, or without risking loss of some of the valued humanness factors commonly associated with face-to-face interactions.

Technology will not replace teachers. But teachers who use technology will replace those who don't.

Christine Meloni

As the capabilities of technology have increased, as more information continues to be created online, and as connections with other people around the world continue to be facilitated, we predict that teachers will adopt more and different technologies, moving them from the realm of simply technology-enhanced toward blended.

> It's not about technology, it's about learning.
>
> Stephen Anspacher

As Neil Selwyn points out, "anyone who is studying education and technology … needs to steer clear of assuming that any digital technology has the ability to change things for the better" (Selwyn 2011, p. 33). **Technology is simply a tool**. The revolution—or, more likely, evolution—will be driven by teachers and learners who recognize that they are in the optimal position to improve education. By intentionally implementing new technology and tools for learning-centered purposes, we can not only adapt to the changing world, but also even increase our ability to both teach and learn.

Blended course development can provide compounding dividends for the institution. Teachers who redesign and teach blended courses can serve as mentors or advisers to other teachers, which can lead to sharing of innovative practices across campus. All of this can add to the institution's body of knowledge and experience supporting good practices in teaching and learning. And, by growing blended courses, an institution may increase its attractiveness to students who increasingly favor blended and online modes.

1.4 Critical Concepts for Blended Course Design

When a course is redesigned as blended, many new possibilities and challenging variables emerge. Among the most important are the concepts of mixing synchronous with asynchronous interactions, planning for learning time, and incorporating the right technologies.

Weaving Synchronous and Asynchronous Interactions

The Internet allows us to communicate with others and access information nearly anywhere and anytime. This facilitates *asynchronous* interactions, which simply means that interactions don't have to happen at the same time. For instance, I can send an electronic message or post comments to a discussion forum whenever I want, and you can read and respond to that in your own time. This provides significant flexibility to teach and learn together, but with different schedules.

The kinds of interaction that happen together in real time are called *synchronous*. In a blended course, synchronous interactions may happen face to face during onsite meetings, or they may happen online, through live chat or videoconferencing.

While any course can incorporate both asynchronous and synchronous interactions, a blended course design can easily choose either. Thus, the course designer should be particularly

Examples of Synchronous and Asynchronous Online Tools

Synchronous
- Web conferencing (e.g. Adobe Connect, GoToMeeting)
- Voice-Over-IP (e.g. Skype, Google Talk)
- Chat, instant messaging

Asynchronous
- Discussion forums
- Email
- Wikis

Mixed
- Text messaging (SMS)
- Twitter
- Facebook, Linkedin, Google+
- Google Docs

aware of the strengths and weaknesses of each. Chapter 3 addresses these kinds of interactions in terms of student engagement, and specific asynchronous and synchronous learning activities are explored in Chapters 7 and 8.

Planning for Learning Time

When a blended course reduces the number of onsite meetings, this opens up that meeting time for online learning experiences (Figure 1.3). For instance, if a Tuesday/Thursday class drops the Thursday onsite session, the teacher might ask, "How will I fill that hour online?" Let's look at that hour not simply as something that will be moved online, but as just another hour in the total learning time of the course. Total learning time includes the time spent in onsite class sessions as well as the time we expect students to use reading, completing assignments, studying, and so on.

A blended course design considers the reduced onsite hour not as an hour lost, but rather *added* to the offsite or online activities students can expect to work through each week. Table 1.1 illustrates this using the standard learning time formula used by many U.S. colleges and universities: for each hour "in class," we expect two to three hours of "study time."

If you calculate the total learning time for your course, mixing both onsite meetings and study time together, the first question in designing a blended course is how often to meet onsite. Meeting onsite one hour per week in a three-credit course results in between eight and eleven hours to be assigned to online or learning activities.

Table 1.1 Expected learning time for a three- and five-credit onsite course in a fifteen-week semester

Course Credits	Learning Time per Week (Hours)		
	Onsite Meetings	Study Time	Week Total
3	3	6–9	9–12
5	5	10–15	15–20

Note that *learning time does not automatically equate to learning*. While time on task is important, some students begin with more background knowledge and experience, and some students learn faster or more efficiently than others.

Indeed, this is one of the advantages of blended learning: online resources and activities do not have to be one-size-fits-all. They can extend beyond the needs of the average student, and provide additional instruction or remediation for students with less background knowledge. Teachers can construct frameworks whereby students engage with the teacher or their peers only as much as they need to. Blending allows students to take some ownership of their learning path, based on assessment of their individual needs.

Metacognition essentially means thinking about thinking. In education, it refers to a process in which learners reflect on what they have learned, identify their own learning gaps, and make plans to address those learning gaps in the future. Metacognition can be encouraged in blended courses in which past learning is made visible to students through their digital footprints in the online course environment.

A blended course is designed within the framework of total learning time. It is equally important to frame the blended course in the context of goals and learning outcomes that describe a successful learner at the end of the course. Assessments and activities will vary in a blended course, and will be based on the most effective use of online technology or onsite meetings, but learning outcomes should be identical to those of the onsite version.

 Learning outcomes for a blended course are identical to those of the onsite version.

Blending in the Right Technologies

A blended course requires an online learning environment to organize and supplement the onsite sessions. The online environment may be a simple website combined with email or discussions. Many institutions will have an LMS that provides a variety of out-of-the-box tools and features that are designed specifically for online activities. Many of the examples in this book illustrate different LMS tools or features; Table 1.2 provides an overview of common LMS tools.

edupunk, n.
A teacher or learner who rejects standardized or corporate teaching tools and practices in favor of independent, individualized, and do-it-yourself methods. Coined by educational technologists Jim Groom and Brian Lamb.

The LMS is not the only toolset at a teacher's disposal. Indeed, technology-enhanced teaching predates the LMS, and many veterans of online education remember using basic websites, emails, and online discussion forums independent of an LMS. In the late 1990s, Web-enhanced teaching was necessarily a do-it-yourself (DIY) endeavor, but nowadays a new DIY ethos has emerged among teachers who wish to break free from the constraints and paradigm of the LMS.

The rise of easy-to-use, freely available Web-based tools for creating, collaborating, and sharing (e.g. blogs, video sharing, wikis, etc.) has introduced teachers to the idea that anyone

Table 1.2 Common features in an LMS

Class Management	Communication and Interaction	Organization and Resources	Practice and Assessment
Class roster	Class announcements	Web page creation	Quizzes and tests
Grade book	Private messaging	Lesson sequencing	Surveys
Group management	Discussion forums	Outcome alignment	Online assignments
Peer review assignments	Live chat	File upload	Self-checks
Data tracking or learning analytics	Videoconferencing	Conditional release	Rubrics
	Multimedia comments	Collaborative editing	
	System notifications	RSS feed aggregation	
	Outgoing RSS feeds		

Web 2.0 simply refers to Web-based tools, services, and websites that allow for user participation and creation of content. Now considered to just be the natural affordances of the Web, the central interest in Web 2.0 has been in the effects and empowerment that comes with freely creating, sharing, and interacting within open, global communities.

can showcase their everyday learning in a space they own and are proud of. These open, online tools and services are authentic and reflect real-world interactions. For example, instead of having students submit assignments to the teacher's drop box via an LMS, students could post their assignments on their own blog or personal website. Teachers then visit that website when the work needs to be assessed. We'll explore this idea further in Chapters 6 and 8.

Discovering new information, thinking critically and reflectively, and sharing through open, online networks is an emerging pattern of engaged, lifelong learning now bolstered by the Web. Blended learning can take advantage of real-world online tools and services to guide students toward habits and practices that will enable them to grow and thrive both within and beyond the boundaries of the classroom.

1.5   Time Expectations for Teachers and Students

Both teachers and students should plan to adapt their normal learning habits in order to succeed in a blended course. This doesn't necessarily mean that teachers and students will spend more time in a blended course; rather, time will be distributed differently throughout a week, depending on the course design.

How is Teacher Time Spent?

There is no "typical" blended course, but you might expect to adapt your time usage as follows:

Daily

- Check for communication from students or notifications from the LMS.
- Identify students struggling to achieve outcomes and intervene.
- Respond to specific questions, either privately (e.g. via email) or for the whole class (e.g. via an online post).
- Read and contribute to online discussions or blogs.

Weekly

- Preview upcoming learning activities.
- Conduct onsite meeting(s) with specific lessons for face to face.
- Create, find, and share new material (as needed) for the course website.
- Provide feedback on student work.
- Enter scores into an online grade book or via assignment submission tools.
- Evaluate the blended design and online tools, and adjust settings as needed.

The constant availability of Internet communication tools allows us to work anytime and anywhere, but that doesn't mean we have to work all the time, everywhere. Throughout this book, we'll offer tips and advice on managing your time efficiently, and avoiding common teaching time sinkholes.

Every course redesign project is a time- and energy-intensive effort, and blended courses are no different. They may require more thoughtful planning than either traditional onsite or fully online courses, as blending allows for a greater number of possible activities. And while online and blended courses may require more upfront work, strategic development of resources and activities can actually reduce time spent once the course is up and running.

Reflection

You've decided to design a blended course, but how much time will it take? Spend a few minutes to realistically assess the time and energy that you can commit to your blended course project. Here are some questions to guide you:

When does the course begin? Figure out how many weeks you have before students will start. That gives you a sense of the timeline for development. You might subtract a week or two to give yourself some latitude.

When will you work on the course? Set aside regular blocks of time every week to devote to the blended course design. This will help you stay on schedule. We recommend blocks of 2–4 hours.

How many lessons will you have to do per week? Focusing on individual lessons provides milestones that can shape your design process. Ideally, you'll be able to work on a single lesson over one or more sessions

When will you have colleagues, students, or others to preview the course website? This is an important step before the course goes live, since it can alert you to any major design gaps in a short amount of time. Do it when possible.

How much time can you spend on revising once the course begins? Some teachers will set aside time each week specifically for revisions. Others will make notes throughout the semester and make all revisions after reflecting on the overall success.

1.6   Summary and Standards

Continual advancements in technology and our connections to the Internet are changing our way of life to the point that we live "blended" with online information and services. Blended learning offers teachers an opportunity to take big strides forward by not just employing technology to fit the changing world, but in fact adapting and redesigning their teaching to produce transformative learning experiences.

A blended course replaces some proportion of onsite learning experience with online experiences. However, good blended learning is not just a digital facelift of the traditional onsite course. Blended learning can create opportunities to bridge formal learning to informal learning, and encourage lifelong learning habits.

Blended courses typically mix synchronous with asynchronous activities. Planning these activities—whether onsite or online—can be based on an estimation of total learning time, rather than merely replacing one or more class sessions with online sessions. This provides a framework for design, but time on task alone doesn't guarantee success. To this end, blended course design should be focused on the same learning outcomes as onsite or online versions.

A variety of technologies can be employed to help learners reach these outcomes, from institutional systems such as LMS, to the real-world online tools and social media services that encourage creating, collaborating, and sharing on the open Web.

☐ Learning outcomes for a blended course are identical to those of the onsite version.

References and Further Reading

Beatty, B. (2007). Transitioning to an online world: Using hyflex courses to bridge the gap. In C. Montgomerie & J. Seale (Eds.), *Proceedings of World Conference on Educational Multimedia, Hypermedia and Telecommunications*, Chesapeake, VA.

Beatty, B. J. (2010). Hybrid courses with flexible participation: The hyflex design. Retrieved from http://itec.sfsu.edu/hyflex/hyflex_course_design_theory_2.2.pdf.

Cambell, G., & Groom, J. (2009). No digital facelifts: Toward a personal cyberinfrastructure. *Conference Presentation: Open Ed 2009*, University of British Columbia, British Columbia, Canada. August 13, 2009.

Collins, A., & Halverson R. (2009). *Rethinking education in the age of technology: The digital revolution and schooling in America*. New York: Teachers College Press.

Cross, J. (2006). *Informal learning: Rediscovering the natural pathways that inspire innovation and performance*. Hoboken, NJ: Pfeiffer.

Garrison, D. R., & Vaughan, N. D. (2008). *Blended learning in higher education: Framework, principles, and guidelines.* Hoboken, NJ John Wiley & Sons.

Graham, C. R., Woodfield, W., & Harrison, J. B. (2013). A framework for institutional adoption and implementation of blended learning in higher education. *Internet and Higher Education.* doi:10.1016/j.iheduc.2012.09.003.

Kaleta, R., Skibba, K., & Joosten, T. (2007). Discovering, designing, and delivering hybrid courses. In A. G. Picciano & C. D. Dziuban (Eds.), *Blended learning: Research perspectives* (pp. 111–143). Needham, MA: Sloan Consortium.

Metros, S. (2011). New IT strategies for a digital society. Keynote presented at Campus Technology Virtual Conference. May 12, 2011.

Olapiriyakul, K., & Scher, J. (2006). A guide to establishing hybrid learning courses: Employing information technology to create a new learning experience, and a case study. *Internet and Higher Education,* 9(4), 287–301.

Prensky, M. (2001). Digital natives, digital immigrants. *On the Horizon,* 9(5), 1–6.

Selwyn, N. (2011). *Education and technology: Key issues and debates.* London: Continuum.

Thomas, D., & Brown, J. S. (2011). *A new culture of learning: Cultivating the imagination for a world of constant change.* Charleston, SC: CreateSpace.

Vai, M., & Sosulski, K. (2011). *Essentials of online course design: A standards-based guide.* New York: Taylor & Francis.

Waters, J. K. (2011) Will the real digital native please stand up? *Campus Technology.* Retrieved from http://campustechnology.com/Articles/2011/10/01/Will-the-Real-Digital-Native-Please-Stand-Up.aspx.

Wiley, D. (2006, February). Higher education: Dangerously close to becoming irrelevant. Session presented at Secretary of Education's Commission on the Future of Higher Education, Panel on Innovative Teaching and Learning Strategies. February 2–3, 2006. Retrieved from www.ed.gov/about/bdscomm/list/hiedfuture/3rd-meeting/wiley.pdf.

Wiley, D., & Hilton, J. (2009). Openness, dynamic specialization, and the disaggregated future of higher education. *International Review of Research in Open and Distance Learning,* 10(5).

Yates, B. A., Bakia, M., Means, B., & Jones, K. (2009). *Evaluation of evidence-based practices in online learning: A meta-analysis and review of online learning studies.* Retrieved from http://edicsweb.ed.gov/edics_files_web/03898/Att_References and Glossary.doc.

| Chapter 2 | # Elements of Blended Courses: A Tour |

Elements of Blended Courses: A Tour

2.1 Considerations for Blended Course Designs

In the best blended learning design, the selection and organization of learning activities and assessments support desired learning outcomes while maximizing the strengths — and minimizing the weaknesses — of both online and onsite environments.

There is no single best model for blended courses. A number of variables specific to technology-enhanced teaching will influence blended course design decisions throughout the process. Some of these must be addressed at one time, for example:

- How much learning time can be onsite versus online?
- What learning theories or teaching philosophy does the teacher subscribe to?
- How literate are teacher and students in these specific technologies?

Other variables may be addressed repeatedly throughout the course design process, such as:

- Which mode — onsite or online — best fits the specific learning outcome(s)?
- Is limited onsite time being used to maximum benefit?
- What available technologies support learning without distracting?

How you answer these questions will influence what assessments, activities, and rhythm you adopt in your blended course design.

The Rhythm of Blended Courses

Every course has a natural rhythm. Traditional courses have a rhythm marked by regular face-to-face, onsite meetings, weekly readings, independent practice, and a midterm and final assessment. The closeness of onsite sessions creates a rather tight, focused rhythm that requires all learners to be in sync.

A blended course also sets a rhythm through onsite meetings, but also allows for more individual student variation in the rhythm, depending on the closeness of the onsite sessions.

Some blended course models frame the course with one opening and one concluding onsite meeting, allowing the bulk of the course activities to happen online in between (Figure 2.1). These course models, sometimes called "multi-modal" or "framed," require that students be in sync by the end of the course, and perhaps for certain online, synchronous activities or milestones.

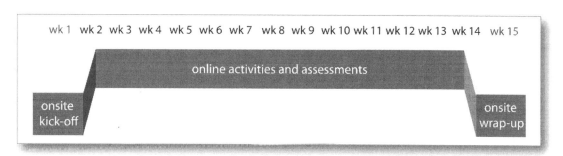

Figure 2.1 Framing a blended course with onsite meetings

Other blended courses provide flexibility within each week by setting the rhythm with weekly onsite meetings (Figure 2.2).

Some teachers who blend courses by moving one or more weekly sessions online will continue to use both days as milestones in the course schedule. For example, a Tuesday/Thursday course keeps only Tuesday sessions onsite, redesigning activities from Thursday sessions for online. The teacher may continue to use Thursday as a milestone in the course schedule, setting due dates or merely recommending

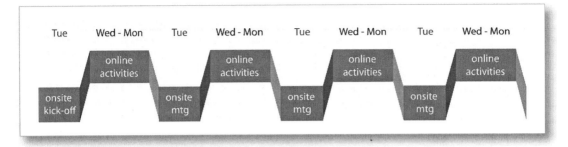

Figure 2.2 Typical rhythm of a week-to-week blended course

personal progress for Thursdays in order to maintain the traditional rhythm of the course.

In any case, because of the added flexibility provided between onsite sessions, blended courses put more responsibility for learning on the students, who must take the initiative to engage in many more online or independent learning activities.

2.2 Blended Course Tours

Let's take a look at three blended course designs that illustrate some of these variables. A deeper analysis of many of the organizational structures, activities, and assessments will be found in the appropriate sections of this guide.

2.3 American Literature since 1865

Course Overview

"American Literature since 1865" is a three-credit university course (forty-five "instructional hours" over fifteen weeks) for both English majors and non-majors. The course aims to develop background knowledge and critical contexts for great American literature and ideas since 1865 through reading, thinking, discussing, and writing.

Focus of the Blend

The blended redesign of this course focuses on taking advantage of the affordances of asynchronous online discussions and digital multimedia to improve student engagement and learning.

Blended Rhythm

The teacher hosts one-hour onsite meetings, once a week, for all fifteen weeks. The activities of these face to face meetings focus on whole-class discussions of the literary works.

Organization

During the first week of class, students are oriented to the course in a live session with the teacher, which allows for discussion of the expectations as described in the syllabus. The teacher knows that students will be expected to interact with each other online, and so he takes some time during that first session to have students meet each other face to face to develop human connections. The first session finishes with the teacher directing students to review the syllabus on the course website independently.

The course website is in a Learning Management System (LMS), and begins with a simple web page as the hub for learning. This online home page is updated each week to direct students to the current week's lesson (Figure 2.3). Each lesson is a highly organized sequence of instructions, materials, and discussion forums, with appropriate hyperlinks to support navigation.

Each lesson is encapsulated in a single web page that:

- introduces the authors for the week with a story or multimedia;
- lists explicit instructions for students to complete the week's activities;
- provides video or audio files that can be downloaded onto a computer or mobile device, or viewed online.

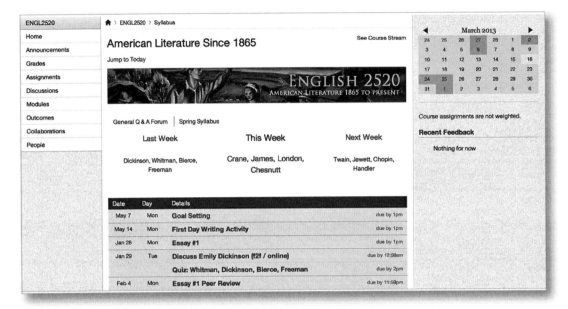

Figure 2.3 The home page in an LMS focuses on the current week in the context of the whole schedule

The lesson's introductory web page is then immediately followed by one or more online discussions (Figure 2.4).

Activities and Assessments

This course uses the following activities throughout:

Independent readings. These are readings of authors' works and related material. Students have access to physical books, but the teacher has also provided links to public domain e-texts on Project Gutenberg when possible.

Project Gutenberg (http://gutenberg. org) is a library of public domain literary works available for download in a variety of formats.

Digital multimedia. This includes audio recordings of authors reading their own works, video clips from stage or screen productions to give context or perspective to authors' works, or segments from documentaries to provide insight into the authors' lives. The multimedia can be accessed online (to stream or download), providing important flexibility to students. Brevity is key, and taking the time to edit down an audio track or video once for online distribution means that the teacher never has to bother—or waste time—queuing up physical media, as is done in traditional onsite classes.

🏠 › ENGL2520 › Pages › Week Two Readings & Resources

Last edited about 1 month ago

ENGLISH 2520
AMERICAN LITERATURE 1865 TO PRESENT

Week Two

Emily Dickinson   Walt Whitman   Ambrose Bierce   Mary Wilkins Freeman

Assignments

This week we focus on Dickinson, Whitman, Bierce, and Freeman. To accomplish this week's goals, you must:

1. **Read** the following:
   a. Emily Dickinson: bio and poems; Norton pp. 74-91
   b. Walt Whitman: "Song of Myself"
   c. Ambrose Bierce: "An Occurence at Owl Creek Bridge"
   d. Mary Wilkens Freeman: "Revolt of Mother"
2. **Study** the author resources (below)
3. **Complete** the practice quiz *before we meet f2f*
4. Discuss authors and works *in-class*
5. **Continue discussion** online

Author Resources

Emily Dickinson

"The Poet in Her Bedroom" is from the TV series "Angles of a Landscape: Perspectives on Emily

Figure 2.4
Each lesson is organized by a page that lists both online and onsite tasks

Author Resources

Emily Dickinson

"The Poet in Her Bedroom" is from the TV series "Angles of a Landscape: Perspectives on Emily Dickinson," which explores little-known aspects of Dickinson's life and work:

Link

Minimize Video

Before we meet...

Does this video give additional insight into why Dickinson chose the subjects she did to write about? Does the domestic context color the way you read any of Dickinson's poems?

Walt Whitman

Walt Whitman's voice is large and apparent even in a silent reading from "Leaves of Grass". In this rare, early recording we can listen to .

Before we meet...

Listening to an author read their own work is a fascinating exercise, because historically, at least, poetry was written to be read aloud. Try reading the poem aloud yourself, then listening to the author. How does the author's reading inform your own? Should we accept the author's oral interpretation of the poem as the only way to read it?

Figure 2.5 Multimedia is embedded directly within the page, with instructions for students on how to use it

Class discussions interwoven between onsite and online environments. Sharing ideas and engaging in critical discussion of texts is a hallmark of literary instruction. Onsite meetings provide a chance for students and teacher to engage in the sensory-rich, highly human face-to-face experience. This helps them to develop a sense of interpersonal empathy and community. Each onsite discussion ends with the teacher reminding students to continue the discussion online.

The online discussions often have a prompt or question, but students can also extend any thread of discussion they may have begun in class. The asynchronous nature of online discussions ensures that every student has a chance—and a responsibility—to respond, and can do so in their own time (Figure 2.6). This also means that students have a chance to further study the literary work, to reflect on each other's ideas, and to compose and edit a thoughtful response.

Essay portfolio with peer reviews. Students' participation in online discussions will lead them to select and refine their best ideas for submission as more formal essays. This is done online, through the LMS's assignments tool, which facilitates the use of rubrics and peer review as well. Rather than the teacher collecting, tracking, and redistributing student essays in-class for peer review, the LMS manages that for him.

The LMS also provides student peer reviewers with the same rubric the teacher will use for his reviews (Figure 2.7). This matches the students' expectations to the peer review experience, and ensures that each student understands the objectives of the essay assignment. This is important, because each essay must be revised based on peer and teacher review feedback. The polished essays are collected in an online essay portfolio at the end of the semester.

Because this is done online and automated by the LMS, precious onsite time is freed up exclusively for discussions.

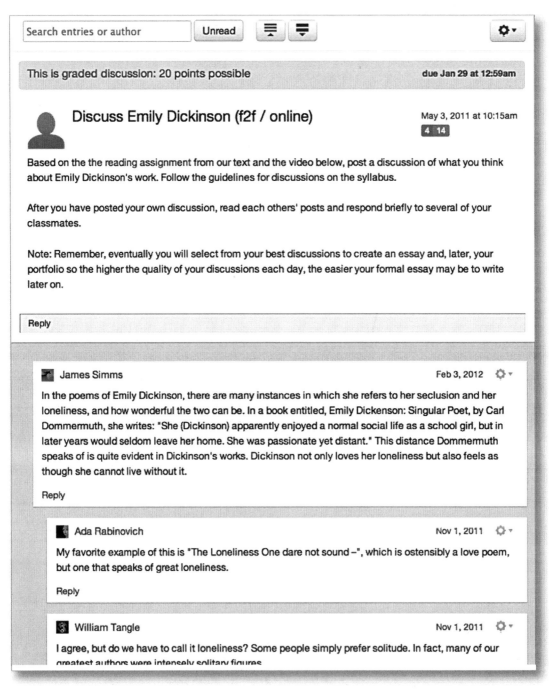

Figure 2.6 Discussions continue to develop online, bridging onsite sessions with asynchronous interaction

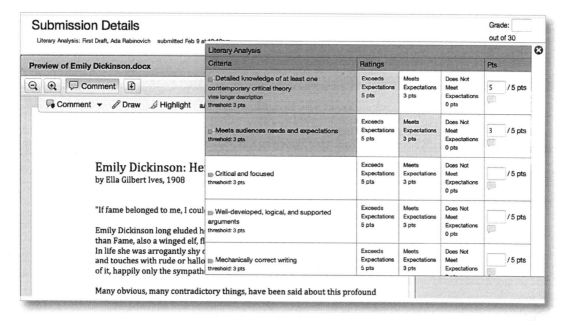

Figure 2.7 Management of peer review is facilitated by the LMS, which manages due dates, submission, distribution, scoring, and interaction

2.4 Introduction to Oceanography

Course Overview

"Introduction to Oceanography" is a four-credit university course (sixty "instructional hours" over fifteen weeks) that introduces majors and non-majors to the history and scientific practice of oceanography. The course was created to intentionally include field trips that would help students connect classroom science to hands-on, physical experiences.

Focus of the Blend

The blended redesign of this course focused on using technology to add flexibility and encourage students to individualize their learning through reusable multimedia and activities. This redesign also involved "flipping" the classroom to make onsite time more engaging and effective.

Accessibility and Universal Design

The "Flipped" Classroom

The idea of a **flipped classroom** turns the traditional lecture and homework model on its head. Rather than having students absorb lectures and explanations during class time, and then sending them home with assignments and practice activities, technology allows teachers to flip these around (Figure 2.8). Lectures are no longer done onsite, but recorded, and put online where students can watch them in their own time, at their own pace, and as many times as needed.

"Homework" is transformed into classwork, where problem-solving and practice activities are supported by direct interaction between students and teacher.

A flipped classroom takes advantage of the Web's ability to serve reusable multimedia to anyone anywhere, while focusing onsite time on the kinds of activities that benefit from individually responsive and fluid interactions.

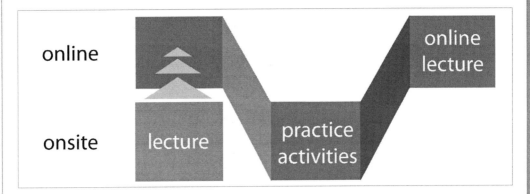

Figure 2.8 A flipped model puts video lectures online and brings the practice activities into the classroom

Blended Rhythm

Introduction to Oceanography meets onsite in a classroom once a week for peer-supported instruction and discussion. It also meets once every three weeks for a three-hour field trip. Online activities are highly organized, but very flexible. Weekly deadlines help students stay on target, but otherwise the time and place of online participation is up to each individual.

Organization

This blended course uses an LMS to organize lessons. The **course home page** reminds students what they need to do each week, with hyperlinks to the appropriate tools where activities take place (Figure 2.9).

A **weekly lesson organizer** begins with a list of required activities and resources to guide students through both online and onsite tasks.

Each week's online lesson includes a **self-check quiz** (see p. 40) that informs the teacher's selection of topics for **onsite peer instruction** activities.

Field trips are organized through the school to locations near the coast, or museums, or laboratories in the area. Instructions for these field trips are provided online.

Figure 2.9 Introduction to Oceanography's home page lists common weekly tasks as well as a list of specific lessons

Activities and Assessments

Independent readings. These come from the required textbook, available in physical form or as an e-text.

Video lectures. Rather than repeatedly delivering lectures each semester to each class, the teacher recorded her

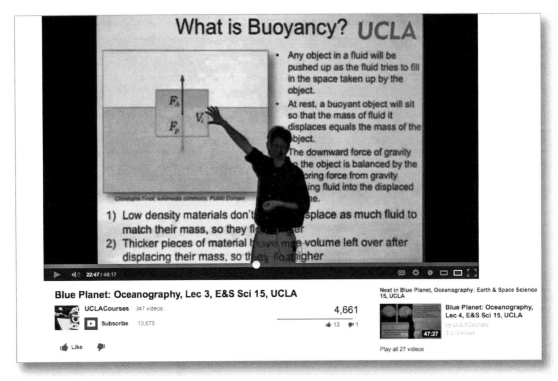

Figure 2.10 This video was produced by UCLA and shared on YouTube. It's just one of many open educational resources that can support a blended course

lectures with any slides or objects used. This was done in her office, using an off-the-shelf webcam and microphone that connected to her computer, and software to create the digital recording.

For some topics, she opted not to record a lecture herself, but used existing lectures by professors at other universities that are openly licensed for reuse (Figure 2.10). These provide variety and alternate perspectives.

When using these third-party lectures, she included a note to students describing where these came from and encouraged them to take the initiative and find other shared media or resources on the open Web.

Self-check quizzes. Each week, students are required to score at least 90 percent on an online quiz. The quiz allows for repeated attempts to provide sufficient opportunity for mastery (Figure 2.11).

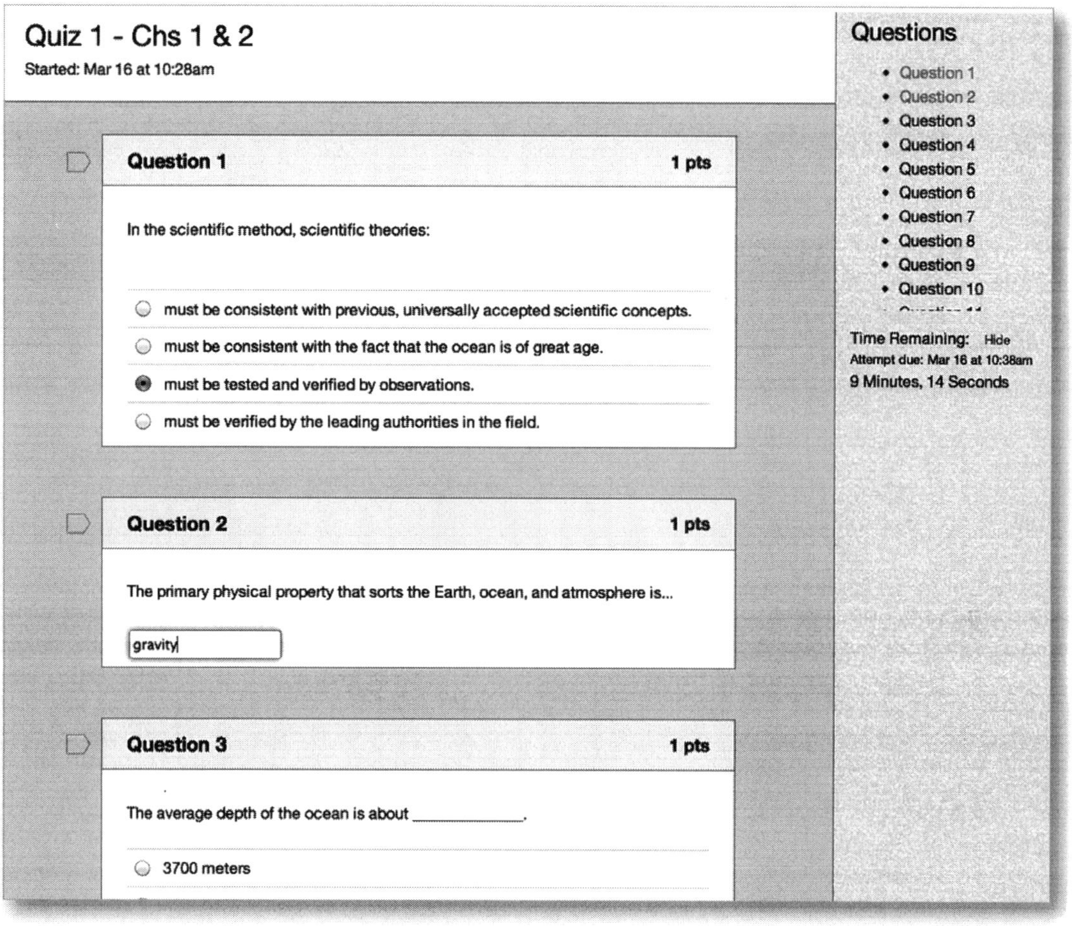

Figure 2.11 Putting self-check quizzes online allows students to take them when they are ready, but before the deadline

Quiz results provide feedback on answer choices to direct students to the appropriate material in the textbook or lecture (Figure 2.12).

Each quiz attempt may deliver different questions than the previous attempt, as the quiz questions are randomly drawn from larger pools of questions kept in an online question bank. This encourages students to do more than just memorize one set of answers; they must actually master the several topics covered by the quiz.

Each week's quiz is due by midnight before the onsite class meeting. This is done so that the teacher can quickly review quiz results online, and identify any particularly troublesome

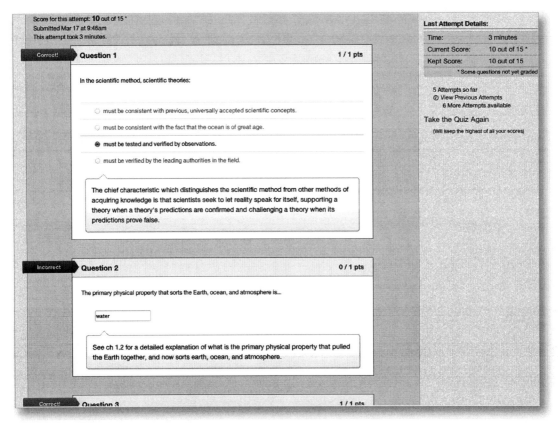

Figure 2.12 Online quizzes provide different kinds of feedback for correct or incorrect answers

questions. She uses these troublesome questions as the focus of onsite, peer instruction activities.

Peer instruction activities. These activities are done onsite, leveraging the synchronous, face-to-face nature of the traditional classroom. The activity itself is based on Eric Mazur's peer instruction model (see Chapter 8 for more on the peer instruction model). The teacher shows a challenging multiple-choice question on the classroom projector. Students register their answer to the question through a wireless "student response system" (aka "clickers"). The results of student responses are immediately available for the teacher. If the class meets the threshold of mastery (85 percent of the class answers correctly), then she moves onto the next question. If not, then she directs students to pair up and discuss and negotiate toward the right answer. After five minutes, students register their answers again, and the cycle repeats until mastery is achieved.

This activity is deemed more engaging and more effective than simple lectures, and takes advantage of several affordances of the onsite environment that provide efficiency that is not easily available online.

Problem set assignments. Students solve and submit problem sets each week through the LMS's online assignments tool. This allows students to not only access instructions and the problems online, but also facilitates submission of digital files.

Field trips. Students work in groups during field trips, and are expected to bring a field notebook and a small video recorder of some type (either one they own, one built into their phone, or one checked out from the department). These are used to record phenomena such as geological formations, tidal patterns, ocean life, etc. The media and notes recorded by the student groups are shared with the class on the online discussion forum (Figure 2.13).

The teacher assesses each group's work based on the media and explanation posted to the forum. This is done using an online rubric that is integrated with the discussion forum through the LMS (see Chapter 6 for more on designing rubrics). Group members can follow up on their original post to provide additional explanation as needed.

Exams. The same pool of questions that are used for weekly quizzes are reused for randomly generated unit exams (four dispersed throughout the semester). Though the exams themselves are online and computer-based, the teacher uses a campus testing center to facilitate the exams. The LMS provides a way for the testing center to lock down all the exams from students who are not properly logged in to the testing center. But by using the LMS, the teacher has access to all students' exam results online, immediately, and is able to track question performance from quizzes to the exam.

Note that because the exams are online, they don't have to be done through the campus testing center, but could be "unlocked" at other approved locations by a proctor. This is often done in fully online courses to ensure exam integrity.

Figure 2.13 The discussion forum provides an online space where students can share the results of onsite activities

2.5 Technology for Elementary Education Teachers

Course Overview

"Integrating Technology for Early Childhood Education" (one credit) and "Integrating Technology for Elementary Education" (one credit) is a two-course sequence intended to help elementary education students to:

- develop technological literacy;
- develop positive dispositions toward educational technology;
- plan effective content-specific technology integration;
- practice technology integration in real-world settings;
- learn about ethical and safe use of technology.

The courses connect closely with other required methods courses that help students to learn how to effectively teach core subjects such as math, language arts, science, social studies, and fine arts.

Focus of the Blend

This course was originally taught as a two-credit hour course with sections of 40–50 students in a traditional face-to-face format. Two of the most significant challenges to teaching this course in the traditional mode were pacing and personalization. Pacing was very difficult because students began the class with a wide range of technical skills. Any pacing we chose for the class would leave a significant number of advanced students bored because the pacing was too slow while others would get lost because we were moving too fast. It was also very difficult to provide personalized instruction to meet individual student needs and misunderstandings in a timely way because of the size of the class. As we considered redesigning the course to address these needs, we also wanted to preserve a high level of teacher–student interaction. We did not want students to feel like they didn't know their instructor and we wanted the instructor to have a positive relationship with each student.

We chose a blended learning redesign in which students were required to attend class onsite the first day of class and the last day of class, as well as a few specific sessions during the semester. Course sessions not designated onsite were online, and during those weeks students could complete all of their coursework through the online activities. Instructors were able to maintain a high level of connectedness with students during the online weeks through weekly video reflection postings where students and teachers communicated using asynchronous video in a weekly discussion space in the LMS.

Asynchronous video

Many LMS discussion boards will allow text postings, audio postings, or video postings to a discussion forum. The use of asynchronous video in discussion forums provides the flexibility of communicating independently of time and place while still allowing participants to experience the human element — vocal and visual communication cues that indicate nervousness, humor, uncertainty, etc. Asynchronous video can help maintain a high level of social presence when teacher and students are separated by time and space.

Additionally, optional face-to-face lab tutorial sessions were provided each online week. Students who felt like they wanted or needed face-to-face help could always come onsite. This allowed advanced learners to progress at their own speed online while learners who wanted more individualized tutoring were able to come onsite for personalized help.

Blended Rhythm

The blended rhythm during the semester was different for each student based on individual needs. Most students interacted with the teacher and other students weekly in a video reflection discussion space and then worked through an online agenda that contained instruction and assignments to be completed during the week. Some students would come to the optional onsite lab session each week and work through their online assignments there where they could easily ask questions directly to the instructor if they got stuck. Other students would do most of their work online and attend onsite only when they felt that it was a more efficient way to solve particular problems they were struggling with.

The blended rhythm for the instructors involved posting prompts to the video reflection space and interacting with students there as they posted their reflections. The instructor would also be available to diagnose problems and provide tutorial help to those who needed it each week during the optional lab sessions. Several times during the semester, the instructor would lead an onsite class session with all of the students present.

Organization

The course uses an LMS to organize all of the course activities. Each week in the course is clearly designated in-class (i.e. onsite) or online (Figure 2.14). Onsite sessions were held at the beginning of the semester so that the students could connect on a personal level with the instructor and peers in the course. The online weeks involved contributing an online video reflection post to the class or group discussion along with project work. The project work was supported through a set of online video tutorials that were created as screencasts.

Screencasting

Screencasting tools allow a teacher to video capture what is happening on the screen. So instead of trying to explain a complex set of maneuvers or instructions in text, the instructor can show the student how to perform the task. Additionally, students can use free screencasting tools to create videos that show instructors what they are doing on the screen when they get stuck with a problem. The screencasts "show" instead of "telling with text," avoiding a lot of miscommunication.

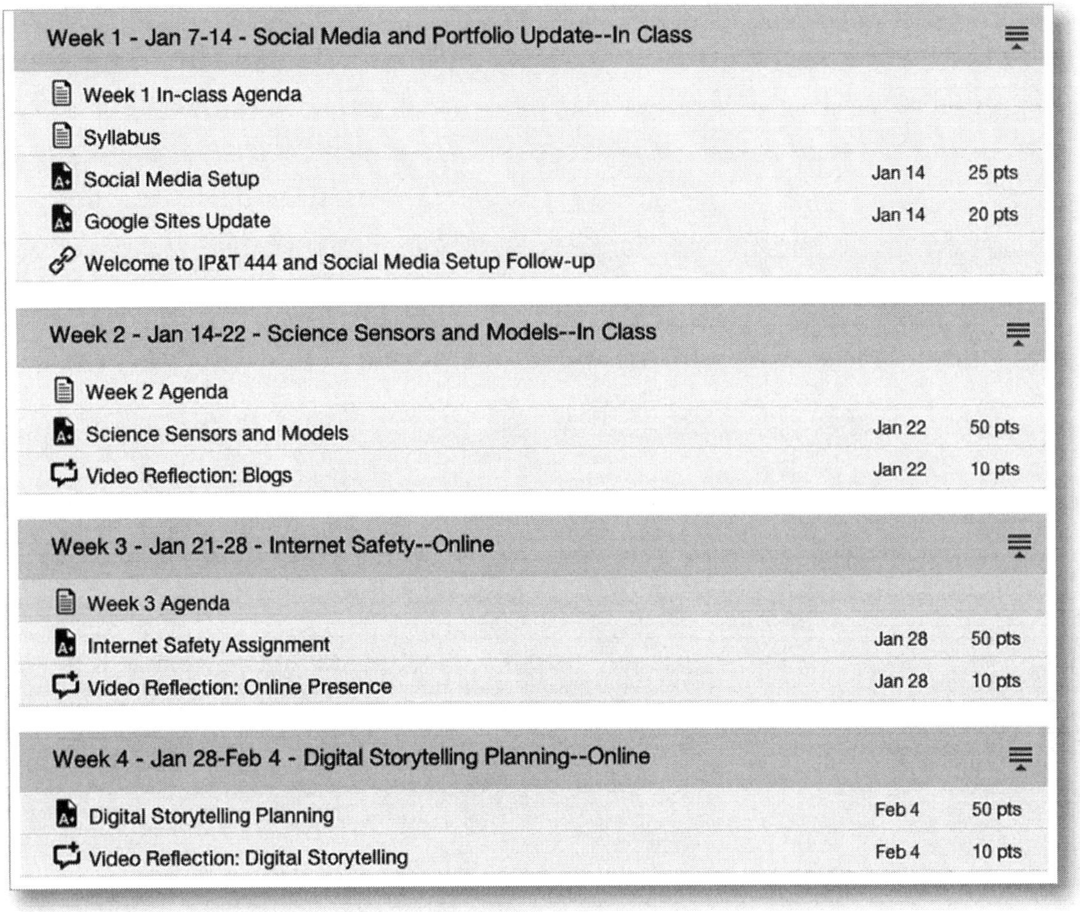

Figure 2.14 The LMS schedule indicates if each week is a required in-class session or if it is online instruction with an optional in-class lab

Activities and Assessments

Pre-post assessments. The course begins with a pre-assessment and ends with a post-assessment that measures change in students' attitudes toward technology and general technology knowledge.

Mid-course evaluation. The institution provides an online mid-course evaluation tool that allows instructors to create questions and receive anonymous feedback from students on the course.

We link to the institution's mid-course evaluation tool on the website.

Figure 2.15 Example of an online student portfolio

Projects and portfolio assessment. The majority of the knowledge and skills in the course are assessed through mastery-based projects that are accumulated into an online portfolio. The online portfolios are created using Google Sites and are owned and maintained by the students (Figure 2.15).

Mastery-based projects have technical requirements that must be met in order to be marked as complete. Students must complete all projects to pass the class. Students lose points on projects by not completing them on time. A project is considered complete on the date that it is submitted with all of the criteria completed.

2.6 Summary

In each of these blended course examples, the design focused on leveraging online technology for its strengths, including centralized organization and structure, reusable multimedia, asynchronous discussion, automated assessment scoring and management, social interaction and community engagement, and student management. Perhaps even more importantly, onsite, face-to-face time is maximized. Onsite activities are redesigned to leverage the strengths of the face-to-face mode, primarily its synchronous nature, the sensory richness, and highly human experiences.

Later chapters will more fully explain the activities and assessments described in these examples as you immerse yourself in the blended course design process. Still, plan to revisit the concrete examples shown in this chapter to help you form strong mental models of how a blended course looks week-to-week, lesson-to-lesson, throughout the term of the semester.

Chapter 3

Engaging Learners in a Blended Course

The engagement of the imagination is the only thing that makes any activity more than mechanical.

John Dewey, *Democracy and Education*

The *3 Es* are commonly used criteria for evaluating the quality of an instructional experience:

- **Effectiveness**—refers to how well students are able to achieve the learning outcomes for a course.
- **Engagement**—refers to the emotional and mental energy that students are willing to expend during a learning experience.
- **Efficiency**—refers to the resources (teacher/student time, effort, money, etc.) invested in the development and implementation of an instructional activity.

This chapter focuses on strategies for designing blended courses that will engage learners. Instruction that does not engage learners will not be effective in the long run. This is especially true in blended courses, as moving activities online may increase the sense of distance between student and classmates.

There are no absolute recipes for engaging all learners. Learners come to the table with different desires, goals, and limitations. One of the strengths of a blended learning environment is that it increases the range of tools and potential strategies that can be used to reach learners. Instruction that takes place both online and face to face can provide a mix of approaches that allows all learners to engage in meaningful ways. Through experience, instructors can learn which combination of approaches works best for different students.

3.1 Engaging Heart and Mind

Any training that does not include the emotions, mind and body is incomplete; knowledge fades without feeling.

Anonymous

Student engagement is the product of motivation and active learning. It is a product rather than a sum because it will not occur if either element is missing.

Elizabeth F. Barkley, *Student Engagement Techniques*

Gin Xin is a student from China in her first year of school at a university in the United States. She feels very confident in her reading and writing ability, but less confident in her ability to communicate orally. She often has good ideas she would like to share during classroom discussion but is reluctant because of the fast pace of discussion and her anxiety about her speaking abilities.

Fortunately, the instructor always extends the classroom discussion after class via an online discussion forum. Gin contributes her ideas to the discussion online, where she has more time to carefully and accurately articulate her ideas. Both her instructor and peers often praise Gin for her valuable contributions to the online conversation. This increases her satisfaction and creates a strong sense of connection between her and her classmates, both of which motivate her continued engagement in course activities.

This highlights two important aspects of learner engagement: engaging learners' hearts and minds. Reaching a learner's heart is often referred to as "affective engagement" and engaging the mind in the content is often called "cognitive engagement."

Reaching hearts is a precondition to learners really engaging in the content with their minds.

A learner who is affectively engaged has a desire to learn and is willing to commit mental effort to the challenging mental tasks required in the learning process. Oftentimes, instruction,

Jorge is a first-year university student enrolled in a college algebra course. He has never considered himself to be good at math—in fact, he struggled all through high school to understand concepts in his math classes. Algebra is a required course for the business degree that he hopes to graduate with and he has convinced himself that he will be satisfied if he can just pass the class with a C grade.

On the first day of class, Jorge is surprised when the instructor begins by telling of a personal experience of a time when she failed her first math exam at the university and thought that the world had ended for her. She explains that algebra is something everyone can learn, and learn well. "Failure is not an option!" she exclaims.

The class will be using a mastery-based approach to learning algebra with a flipped classroom. Each exam can be taken as many times as needed to reach the 90 percent proficiency level. An online tutorial system is available for use outside of class. Students use the system to learn about and do practice problems for each algebra concept. The instructor monitors student performance on practice problems within the system and then schedules targeted in-class tutorial sessions to work through and explain problems that students are struggling with.

Because his teacher expressed a thorough commitment to the success of each student, Jorge left the first day of class energized and more willing to commit effort to learning algebra.

particularly online instruction, tries to focus entirely on the cognitive (mind) aspects of learning and overlooks the affective (heart) element of learning.

We sometimes assume that learners need to arrive with sufficient desire and self-motivation to learn. But that is not always the case, even with adult learners. Some learners need the help of the instructor and classmates to increase their passion, desire, and confidence for learning.

Online and onsite instruction support different kinds of interactions between learners and content. One mode of instruction may support cognitive or affective outcomes better than another. In the algebra scenario above, the instructor had decided to use face-to-face instruction to share her personal experiences with failure and to express encouragement and confidence in the students' ability to succeed. The online instruction was geared toward providing personalized practice and feedback opportunities for the students. For each unique context, there may be some kinds of outcomes that are more efficiently achieved online and others that are more effectively achieved face to face.

Personal Perspective

Charles R. Graham: Technology for Teachers as a Blended Course

Early in my teaching career, I taught a class to help elementary school teachers learn how to use technology in their future classrooms. I didn't understand the need to engage both students' hearts and minds. I set up activities that ensured every student could master the knowledge and skills to use technology in their classroom once they graduated.

You can imagine my surprise at the end of the semester when many of the course evaluation comments said, in effect, "I know how to do many things with computers now, but I don't like technology and will never use it in my future classroom."

I felt devastated. I was so focused on getting every teacher to demonstrate the knowledge and skills that I neglected the dispositions that the teachers were developing along the way. I had helped students to achieve the cognitive outcomes for the course, but those outcomes were meaningless without the accompanying affective outcomes. In future semesters, I focused more energy in the class on reaching students' hearts by helping them to develop a passion for the effective uses of technology in the classroom and a desire to try new and challenging things in their future classrooms.

3.2 Creating Engagement through Learner Interaction

> Frequent student–faculty contact *in and out of class* is a most important factor in student motivation and involvement. Faculty concern helps students get through rough times and keep on working. Knowing a few faculty members well enhances students' intellectual commitment and encourages them to think about their own values and plans.
>
> Chickering & Gamson (1987, p. 3, emphasis added)

There are three general categories of interaction that can be built into any learning activity. Learners can interact directly with the instructor, with other learners, or with content materials. Each of these types of interaction contributes to the learning experience in different ways. **Instructional activities that use a mix of different types of interaction will generally be more engaging** than activities that focus predominantly on only one form of interaction.

- **Student–instructor interaction.** This is the interaction that a student has with the instructor. This interaction can be one-on-one, as might occur during office hours or in a personal email exchange. It can also be one-to-many, as when one instructor interacts with a group of students in a classroom lecture and discussion.
- **Student–student interaction.** Interaction between learners can happen informally (e.g., self-organized study groups) or it can be a formal part of a course with classroom discussions, debates, group projects, etc.
- **Student–content interaction.** Interaction with content has traditionally involved reading textbooks and other text-based materials. Now students may also have access to digital content in the form of videos, animations, simulations, etc., all accessible on the open Web.

Human interaction (instructor or peer interaction) and content interaction both have strengths and limitations when it comes to engaging learners. Table 3.1 highlights some of the strengths and limitations that can be considered as an

Physical Distance versus Psychological Distance

One of the reasons why student–instructor and student–student interaction can be so powerful is because of the instructor or peer's ability to connect on an emotional level with students. Michael Moore, an early distance educational researcher, recognized this and developed the "theory of transactional distance."

This theory helps us to understand that physical distance is not as important as psychological distance when it comes to engaging learners. For example, a student might feel emotionally closer to an online instructor on the other side of the world who he interacts with personally than to a classroom instructor with 200 students who develops no personal relationship with the students during a semester.

appropriate mix of human and content interaction is being designed into a course.

Notice from Table 3.1 that the strengths and weaknesses of human and content interaction oftentimes complement each other. This means that appropriately designed course blends can take advantage of the strengths of both types of interaction to help engage learners in the instruction.

☑ Online or onsite modes are chosen by how their qualities best support learning activities and outcomes.

☑ Human interaction is used to increase emotional engagement when appropriate.

☑ Learning activities and lesson plans allow the teacher to increase personal interaction with struggling students.

Caution: It is also possible to design instruction that focuses on human and content interactions in their areas of weakness. In this case, instead of getting a blend that is the "best of both worlds," a blend that is the "worst of both worlds" is generated.

Table 3.1 Some strengths and limitations of human versus content interaction

	Strengths	Limitations
Human Interaction	**Emotions**. Humans can connect on an emotional level (love, empathy, concern, etc.). Humans can be very effective at conveying excitement or passion for a topic that is contagious. **Complex Diagnostics**. Humans with content expertise are good at quickly diagnosing where problems are in a student's learning.	**Patience/Consistency**. Humans are not good at repeating the same instruction and/or feedback over and over consistently. They get bored, lose interest, and/or begin to make mistakes. **Access/Availability**. It is difficult for a person to multitask in a way that serves many diverse student needs at the same time. People also don't want to be available twenty-four hours a day.
Content Interaction	**Patience/Consistency**. Computers can repeat the same instruction or feedback over and over exactly the same without tiring or making mistakes. **Access/Availability**. Content interactions can be available to the learner twenty-four hours a day, whenever the learner needs or wants it. Machines can multitask to serve multiple students simultaneously.	**Emotions**. Computers and/or static content aren't agents that possess emotion, so it is difficult to connect with learners on an emotional level. **Complex Diagnostics**. Computers are getting better at complex diagnostics—especially where large populations are concerned. However, they still have a difficult time diagnosing and providing feedback on complex learning tasks.

3.3 Designing Human Interaction to Engage Learners

> Good teaching cannot be reduced to technique; good teaching comes from the identity and integrity of the teacher.
>
> Parker J. Palmer

Online interaction can amplify the characteristics of an instructor whether they be good or bad. For example, an instructor who is interested in building relationships with students and providing help to them on a personal level will find many new ways to connect online. Alternatively, an instructor who delivers a boring dispassionate lecture in class or is not interested in personal interactions with students is not

Khan Academy and the Flipped Classroom. Khan Academy (www.khanacademy.org) was built to facilitate the flipped classroom (see Chapter 2). The site has thousands of video tutorials teaching specific skills, predominantly in math and science (Figure 3.1). The site aims to support self-directed learning, but can also be incorporated into blended course lesson plans by teachers.

At Khan Academy, students select a skill they are interested in learning, and interact with practice problems and supporting tutorial videos. Data related to student performance are collected and made available to the instructor who will follow up in class with additional instruction and practice.

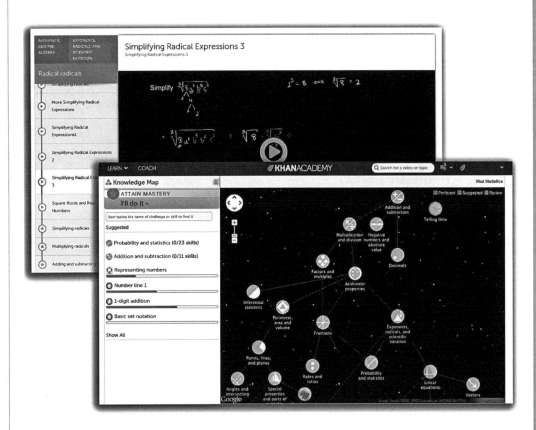

Figure 3.1 Self-paced tutorials and videos at www.khanacademy.org

likely to create engaging lecture videos to share with students online or reach out to students using online communication tools.

Onsite Interaction

Onsite instructor and peer interaction form the core of the traditional course experience. In most classes, the majority of time is spent in lectures with the instructor delivering content. A lecture might be augmented with time for student questions or classroom discussion. In general, learners will be more engaged if they have greater opportunities to be active participants in class rather than just passive consumers of course content.

There are many challenges in the traditional classroom that limit what an instructor can do to engage *all* students in the learning. Table 3.2 presents several of these challenges to engagement and the limitations that are encountered in a traditional face-to-face classroom setting.

Online Interaction

Online interaction isn't constrained by time and place, and is thus free from many of the limitations of onsite interactions (Table 3.2). Table 3.3 describes how online instruction can be used to complement onsite instruction by addressing its limitations.

Tip

Personal relationships can develop more quickly in a face-to-face setting. By preceding online interactions with onsite interactions, a blended course can establish personal connections and a sense of community that fosters deep online discussions.

- **Synchronous**—instruction that occurs in real time (e.g. a phone conversation is synchronous).
- **Asynchronous**—instruction that does not occur in real time (e.g. an email exchange is asynchronous).

At one point in the past, online interactions were only text-based. This meant that online interaction was typically done using email or a text-based discussion board, which prevented much of the power and emotion of conversations to be felt

Table 3.2 Some limitations to learner engagement in a traditional face-to-face classroom setting

Onsite Limitations	
Participation	Time constraints in a physical classroom may make it difficult for everyone to participate or contribute to a discussion. This is particularly the case in sections with large numbers of students. Good instructors address the participation challenge by dividing the class into smaller discussion groups or partner-sharing arrangements.
Pacing	Especially in larger traditional classes, it is often difficult to match your instructional pace with your individual students' ability to learn the material. Instructors usually compromise by pacing the course to the majority of students in the middle, which still leaves the lower students behind and the advanced students bored.
Personalization	Students have a variety of learning preferences that can be difficult for teachers to address when everyone is taught together at the same time.
Place (Authenticity)	Because instruction is confined to a specific space and time, authentic learning activities and assessments can be difficult to design for the classroom. For example, consider how you might provide authentic practice in disciplines such as nursing, teaching elementary school, language learning, etc. if you were not constrained to seat time in a traditional classroom.
Personal Interaction	Even in smaller traditional classes, it can be difficult for the instructor to set aside time for personal one-on-one interaction with her students. Instructor office hours that set aside time for personal interaction with students often conflict with student work.
Preparation	It can be difficult or time-consuming in class for instructors to assess students' understanding of homework activities in order to modify the lesson in real time to meet student needs.

online. More recent technological advances have allowed those at a distance to interact with each other using text, audio, or video either synchronously or asynchronously.

Blending Online and Onsite Discussions and Other Interactions

There are strengths and limitations to using any specific instructional strategy online or onsite. Once these strengths and weaknesses have been identified, the interaction can be

Table 3.3 Some ways that online instruction can be used to address limitations to online learner engagement

	Online Capabilities
Participation	Because online discussions can be done asynchronously, 100 percent of students in a class can be expected to participate in an online discussion.
Pacing	The pacing for online instruction can vary for each student. So a student who does not understand a particular concept can review the material multiple times before moving on.
Personalization	In the online environment, students can be provided with different learning options that best match their learning preferences.
Place (Authenticity)	Blended learning courses can turn authentic contexts into learning spaces. For example, live video might be used to virtually transport the classroom to a place of interest. Additionally, students might physically go to authentic locations and use mobile devices to communicate from those locations with instructors and other class members.
Personal Interaction	One-to-one online interactions via email, texting, or video chat are students' preferred ways to communicate personally with instructors. These ways of communicating are flexible and meet their needs.
Preparation	Online assessments can be used to control real-time access to content or progress in a course. Additionally, access to data from online assessments can provide data that help guide instructors' planning for in-class sessions.

designed to take advantage of the strengths of both environments. For example, Table 3.4 highlights strengths and weaknesses for both face-to-face and online asynchronous discussions. A course that only uses one or the other may not be able to engage all of the learners in the way that a blend of the two can.

Chapter 8 provides additional examples and direction for creating learning activities that engage students with peers and others in their learning community.

 Discussions are designed to capitalize on the asynchronous nature of online and the synchronous nature of onsite.

Table 3.4 Some of the strengths and weaknesses of (primarily asynchronous) online and face-to-face discussions (Graham 2006, p. 18)

	Onsite (Face-to-Face)	Online (Asynchronous)
Strengths	**Human Connection.** It is easier to bond and develop a social presence in a face-to-face environment. It makes it easier to develop trust. **Spontaneity.** It allows for the generation of rapid chains of associated ideas and serendipitous discoveries.	**Flexibility.** Students can contribute to the discussion at the time and place that is most convenient for them. **Participation.** All students can participate because time and place constraints are removed. **Depth of Reflection.** Learners have time to more carefully consider and provide evidence for their claims and provide deeper, more thoughtful reflections.
Weaknesses	**Participation.** It is not always possible to have everyone participate, especially if the class is large and/or there are dominating personalities. **Flexibility.** There is limited time, which means that you may not be able to reach the discussion depth that you would like.	**Spontaneity.** It does not encourage the generation of rapid chains of ideas and serendipitous discoveries. **Procrastination.** There may be a tendency toward procrastination. **Human Connection.** The medium is considered to be impersonal, which may cause a lower satisfaction level when communicating.

3.4 Designing Content Interaction to Engage Learners

Student–content interaction can engage learners in a very different way from student–instructor or student–student interaction. An advantage to building engaging content interaction into a blended course is that computers and the internet are available all hours of the day and night; they never tire of giving the same feedback over and over to students who need it, and, unlike humans, they can provide individualized experiences to many students simultaneously.

Examples of Blended Discussions

Face-to-face first followed by online discussion. An instructor chooses to take advantage of the human connection and spontaneity of face-to-face discussions to start off a classroom discussion. Beginning the discussion in class gets the students excited about the discussion and primes them for the key issues that will drive the discussion. However, everyone is not able to contribute to the discussion in the amount of time available in class. After class, the discussion moves online where **everyone** is expected to build on the discussion that occurred in class.

Online discussion first followed by face-to-face. An instructor has a limited time in class for discussion and wants the discussion to be as powerful as it can. She begins the discussion online a week ahead of time. Everyone must do the reading to prepare in order to contribute meaningfully to the online discussion. The instructor is able to discern from the discussion what the critical areas for classroom discussion are and which students might be called on to participate in the face-to-face discussion wrap-up. The classroom discussion is much richer than it might have been because the students have come to class with ideas and opinions about the topic since they have been discussing it online already for the past week.

You can think of student–content interaction in two general categories: interaction with *static* content and interaction with *dynamic* content.

- **Static content** doesn't change or adapt to input from a student. Examples include e-books, web pages, online videos, and visual images.
- **Dynamic content** changes by reacting to interaction or input from students. Examples include animations, simulations, and online tutorial systems that provide instructional feedback.

Chapter 7 focuses on developing content-driven learning activities that go beyond static content and focus on applying learning.

3.5 Summary and Standards

Engaging a student's heart and mind is essential to a quality learning experience. High levels of engagement result from opportunities for interaction between the student and peers, the instructor, and well-designed content. Blended learning can provide a range of learning activities that build on the strengths of both onsite and online interaction.

Keep these principles of engagement in mind as you begin designing your blended course. Don't forget that in addition to the cognitive outcomes of the mind, we are obliged to also consider how the affective factors (i.e. the heart) play a significant role in teaching and learning.

☐ Online or onsite modes are chosen by how their qualities best support learning activities and outcomes.

☐ Human interaction is used to increase emotional engagement when appropriate.

☐ Learning activities and lesson plans allow the teacher to increase personal interaction with struggling students.

☐ Discussions are designed to capitalize on the asynchronous nature of online and the synchronous nature of onsite.

References and Further Reading

Barkley, E. F. (2010). *Student engagement techniques: A handbook for college faculty*. San Francisco: Jossey-Bass.

Borup, J., West, R. E., & Graham, C. R. (2013). The influence of asynchronous video communication on learner social presence: A narrative analysis of four cases. *Distance Education*, 34(1), 48–63.

Chickering, A. & Gamson, Z. (1987). Seven principles of good practice in undergraduate education. *AAHE Bulletin*.

Dewey, J. (1916). *Democracy and education: An introduction to the philosophy of education*. New York: Macmillan.

Graham, C. R. (2006). Blended learning systems: Definition, current trends, and future directions. In C. J. Bonk & C. R. Graham (Eds.),

Handbook of blended learning: Global perspectives, local designs (pp. 3–21). San Francisco, CA: Pfeiffer Publishing.

McDowell, J. (2011). Using asynchronous video technologies to enhance learner engagement with formative feedback. *ALT-C 2011: Thriving in a colder and more challenging climate.* Retrieved from http://eprints.hud.ac.uk/10888/.

Merrill, M. D. (2008). Reflections on a four decade search for effective, efficient and engaging instruction. In M. W. Allen (Ed.), *Michael Allen's 2008 e-learning annual* (Vol. 1, pp. 141–167). Hoboken, NJ: Wiley Pfieffer.

Merrill, M. D. (2009). Finding e3 (effective, efficient and engaging) instruction. *Educational Technology*, 49(3), 15–26.

Moore, M. G. (1993). Three types of interaction. *Distance education: New perspectives* (p. 19). New York: Routledge.

Moore, M. G. (2007). A theory of transactional distance. In M. G. Moore (Ed.), *Handbook of distance education* (2nd ed., pp. 89–105). Mahwah, NJ: Lawrence Erlbaum Associates.

Chapter 4

Designing Blended Courses

Creativity is allowing yourself to make mistakes. Design is knowing which ones to keep.

Scott Adams

A clear and simple process can guide your design decisions each step of the way. It can ensure that the resulting blended course is learning-centered and takes advantage of opportunities for ongoing improvements.

4.1 Rethinking Course Design

You start with a course. It may be one that you've taught before, or it may be entirely new to you. Your institution may have offered the course in the past. There may be a standard textbook, materials, and assessments from past semesters.

When approaching blended teaching with an established course, the redesign strategy may seem obvious: simply decide which onsite activities can be moved online. Unfortunately, **simply replicating onsite activities online will not yield the best results**. In the worst case, the resulting blended course will not measure up to the rigor, engagement, or outcomes of the onsite course.

This is just one of the common pitfalls of blended course design. Others include:

- **Creating "a class and a half."** It is quite possible to create too much work for students by simply *adding* online or onsite activities to an existing course design. A blended redesign should *replace*.
- **Unfocused technology.** Using technology simply for technology's sake may actually interfere with students' progress toward learning outcomes. Instead, focus on learning outcomes every step of the way.

- **Misfit modes.** Some onsite activities may be misfits in online environments, and forcing a fit will ignore opportunities for transformative redesign. Instead, a blended course design is based on a rethinking of the entire instructional approach.

Personal Perspective

Jared Stein: Web Design as a Blended Course

My first truly blended course was a redesign of a fully *online* course that I'd taught for years. At first, I thought I could simply repurpose the existing online course 100 percent, using the once-a-week onsite sessions as open discussions to clarify or explore topics that interested students. But leaving the onsite sessions open didn't produce the results I wanted; many students came to class expecting to hear lectures and explanations that *were already online*. A few rightfully complained that the class sessions were a waste of time since they'd already completed related online activities.

I recognized that I needed to fundamentally rethink what I was doing in those onsite sessions, so:

- I kept the online lesson review quizzes, but moved due dates to just before the start of each onsite meeting. This ensured that students had some experience with the material before we met.
- I looked closely at the course outcomes and corresponding online activities, and considered which could be done more effectively onsite. I ended up dropping certain online activities entirely to create hands-on or small group activities. For example, an online video followed by discussion about usability testing was transformed into a mock usability test in class: the class collaborated on the selection of usability evaluation items, then students partnered with each other to observe their interaction with randomly selected websites.
- I reserved time at the end of each class session for live troubleshooting. Any student could email his weekly project ahead of the onsite session with a question. I would walk through the troubleshooting process aloud, regularly enlisting the class's help. This provided a kind of *cognitive apprenticeship* that helped students understand the solution and adopt similar troubleshooting strategies themselves.

A blended course is the same amount of work as online or onsite versions.

 Online or onsite modes are chosen by how their qualities best support learning activities and outcomes.

Simplifying Course Design by Going "Backward"

There is considerable intuitive appeal to the concept of integrating the strengths of synchronous and asynchronous (text-based Internet) learning activities. At the same time, there is considerable complexity in its implementation with the challenge of virtually limitless design possibilities and applicability to so many contexts.

Garrison and Hanuka (2004)

In order to avoid common pitfalls, a blended course must, first and foremost, be **learning-centered**. This means that teacher and students have shared goals to achieve a specific set of learning outcomes, and work together to achieve those outcomes.

Teachers provide structure, interactions, activities, and feedback that focus students on their learning and support their progress toward goals. These are the fundamental elements of course design.

Learning-Centered

As an alternative to "learner-centered", the phrase "learning-centered" acknowledges the teacher's critical role in shaping the goals and activities that lead to learning without diminishing the importance of the learner (Anderson, 2008)

A teacher is best guided by a clear vision of a successful student and the knowledge, skills, attitudes, and abilities that she evidences at the end of the course. In short, we must begin with the end in mind.

This means we must first identify learning goals and **outcomes**. Attainment of outcomes is measured, and feedback is provided through carefully designed **assessments**. Students will only be prepared to perform well on those assessments by way of meaningful **learning activities**— focused experiences that build knowledge, develop skill, and shape behavior or attitudes. Figure 4.1 illustrates the direction of this process.

This "backward" design approach may seem counterintuitive at first, but think about anything that you've successfully learned to do. Don't you always have to begin with the end in mind?

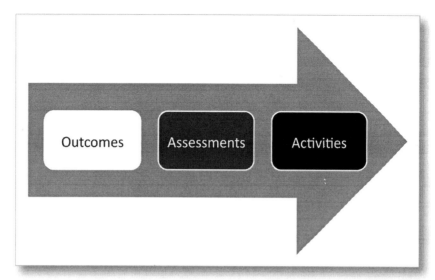

Figure 4.1 The three stages of backward design of a learning experience

Tip

Teachers who already have a syllabus for the onsite version of their course will be able to use it for key information during the design process from day one as they aim to understand desired learning outcomes in the context of the syllabus, textbook, and other pre-existing material. Just remember that **a syllabus for an onsite course is not a blueprint for a blended course**, and may in fact limit your view of what is possible in a blended course.

When you start a project or task, don't you always have some idea of what the result or outcome will be? Isn't there always some way that you or others determine whether you've been successful? And doesn't it always take work, practice, or experimentation to get you there?

Experienced teachers will implicitly know what the desired learning outcomes are for their students, but they may not be able to articulate them. Having clearly articulated, measurable learning outcomes from the beginning of the design process will help ensure that all assessments and activities are *aligned* with the educational goals. Assessments that are aligned will most accurately determine the degree to which learners have achieved outcomes. Alignment helps us in three ways:

- **Alignment keeps course design efforts more manageable** by focusing the teacher on only critical outcomes.
- **Alignment makes learning time more efficient** by limiting the scope of learning activities.
- **Alignment results in better learning outcomes** by ensuring that what we measure is what was taught (Cohen 1987).

☑ Resources and activities support learning outcomes.

☑ Assessments determine the degree to which learners have achieved the required learning outcomes.

Another aspect of this process that may seem backward is that we discourage teachers from focusing on the syllabus at step one, but rather build the syllabus in progressively, after first identifying course goals and outcomes (Chapter 5) and designing one or more lessons (Chapters 6–9).

This design approach provides useful stages for the design and development of learning outcomes, assessments, and activities (see Figure 4.2). This guide focuses on applying these stages as steps in constructing one lesson at a time.

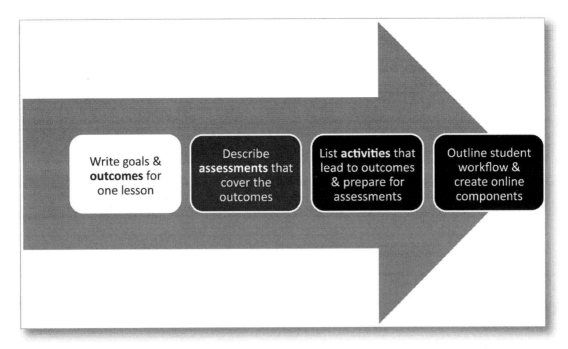

Figure 4.2 Simple steps for a backward design of a single lesson

To help you work through your blended course design process, we provide a **course design map template** that will help you plan your blended course. Use the template in conjunction with Chapters 5–8 to guide your design of individual lessons.

 Find the course design map template—and other great design resources—on the website.

Table 4.1 The planning worksheet helps you stage critical elements of each lesson

Lesson Title: Course Orientation		
Goal:		
Outcomes	**Assessments**	**Activities**
Course Orientation Goal: Prepare to engage in the course		
• Understand course parameters and expectations • Recognize classmates and join a team • Become familiar with course website and tools	• 100 percent on syllabus quiz (online) • Team sign-up (online) • Introductions in forum (online)	• Meet and greet and overview (face to face) • Read syllabus (online) • Explore course site (online)
Lesson title *Lesson goal(s)*		
1. Outcome(s) 2. ...	1. Online or face-to-face assessment(s) 2. ...	1. Online or face-to-face activities 2. ...

Ultimately, blended course lessons will be constructed online, even though some activities will take place onsite. The *online* lesson may consist of:

- A module or folder to organize and sequence the activities (Figure 4.3).
- Introductory page(s) explaining the lesson, indicating outcomes, and providing resources.
- Online discussion forums, quizzes, assignments, or other online activities.

Focusing on one lesson at a time will help you quickly develop working versions of learning experiences with the intent to immediately evaluate, improve, and learn from those improvements in subsequent versions of the lesson. We refer to this as the strategy of **iterative development**.

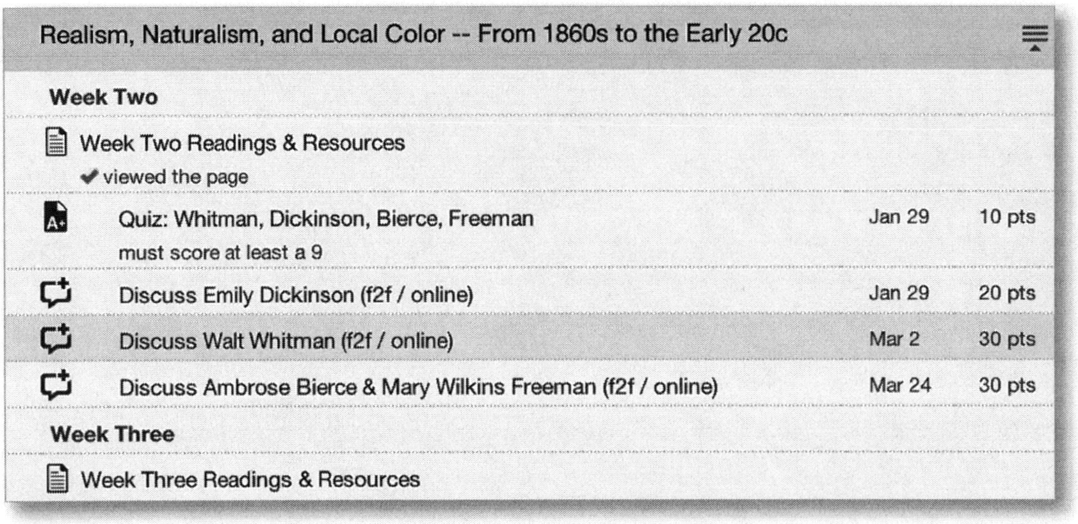

Figure 4.3 Organization of a single lesson within an LMS

4.2 A Strategy of Iterative Development

Iterative development bolsters the backward design approach for individual learning activities, lessons, or units by emphasizing ongoing improvement through three activities:

1. **Designing.** Create a version of a lesson using backward design.
2. **Engaging.** Students learn by working through the blended lesson as the teacher facilitates.
3. **Evaluating.** Examine the results of and feedback on the design. What changes—onsite or online—can improve the design?

In this model, *engaging* students in the learning experience leads to an *evaluation* of the course's effectiveness. Evaluations support a revision or alteration of the lesson *design* (Figure 4.4).

This model process is particularly effective with blended course design because:

- most teachers need to ease into blended design;
- there are so many possibilities—both online and onsite —that the best method may not be obvious the first time.

Figure 4.4
The iterative cycle will help teachers implement design faster, and improve the blend over time

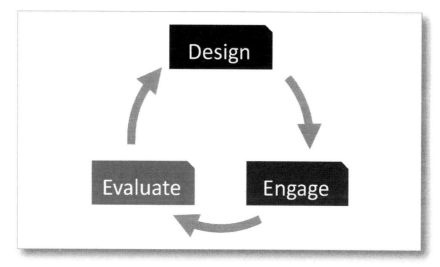

Revising a Field Trip Assignment through Several Iterations

"Introduction to Oceanography" brings students to five different locations for field trips during the semester. Each field trip requires students, working in groups, to document discoveries based on material covered so far.

The first version of the online portion of this activity simply had students submit their findings online for teacher review.

However, the teacher found that the quality of the submissions was mixed, and that students were missing out on the opportunity to learn from the other groups' findings.

Week 1 Field Trip Log Assignment

Due Jan 18 by 10:59pm   **Points** 10

During each field trip, your group will be required to find, document, and share some aspect of the environment (I'll give specific instruction on what to look for when we're onsite). Here's how to proceed from there:

1. During the field trip, **record a short video of your finding.**

2. **Upload your video** to this assignment. If you don't include a detailed description of your finding in the video itself, write one up. Refer to the field log guide for more info.

Figure 4.5 The first version of this assignment has students submitting their findings to the teacher

So, she first added a rubric that clarified the expectations. Then, using the peer review feature of the Learning Management System, she revised the assignment to require groups to also review each other's findings using the same rubric she would use.

After teaching the course for several semesters, the teacher heard from students via a survey that: (1) topic-based online discussions in the course were not always useful for reinforcing learning; and (2) they found great value in viewing each other's work in the field trip peer reviews.

Week 1 Field Trip Log Assignment

Due Jan 18 by 10:59pm   **Points** 10

During each field trip, your group will be required to find, document, and share some aspect of the environment (I'll give specific instruction on what to look for when we're onsite). Here's how to proceed from there:

1. During the field trip, **record a short video of your finding.**

2. **Upload your video** to this assignment. If you don't include a detailed description of your finding in the video itself, write one up. Refer to the field log guide for more info.

3. After the due date, you will receive 2 submissions from other groups to review using the attached rubric (see <u>online guide to completing peer reviews</u>).

Be sure to sign up for your group *before* joining us on the field trip if you haven't already. Use the <u>course calendar</u> to check dates and times.

Field Trip Log Rubric					
Criteria	Ratings				Pts
Discovery is relevant and interesting	Exactly relevant and very interesting in context of this week's lesson. 3 pts		Partly relevant or interesting in context of this week's lesson. 2 pts	Lacks relevance or interest. 1 pts	3 pts
Discovery is thoroughly described view longer description	Detailed and accurate description 4 pts	Generally accurate description 3 pts	Important details are missing from description 2 pts	Generally incomplete or inaccurate description 1 pts	4 pts
Discovery is documented with video	Video completely captured discovery 3 pts	Video mostly captured discovery 2 pts	Video failed to capture significant features of discovery. 1 pts		3 pts
				Total Points: 10	

Figure 4.6 This iteration of the field trip assignment adds a rubric and requires peer review

So she decided to reduce the number of topic-based online discussions, and transform the field trip peer review assignment into an open discussion where students post their findings for the entire class to see and comment on.

While for this latest revision the assignment did sacrifice some of the formal, rubric-based evaluation gained in the limited peer reviews, the teacher found that groups ended up getting *more* feedback from their classmates, and the feedback led to meaningful discussions, rather than just simply comments.

Search entries or author | Unread

This is graded discussion: 10 points possible   due Jan 18 at 10:59pm

Week 1 Field Trip Log Assignment

During each field trip, your group will be required to find, document, and share some aspect of the environment (I'll give specific instruction on what to look for when we're onsite). Here's how to proceed from there:

1. During the field trip, **record a short video of your finding.**

2. **Upload your video** here as part of a new post. If you don't include a detailed description of your finding in the video itself, write one up. Refer to the field log guide for more info.

3. **Respond to the other groups' postings** (at least twice) during the 2 weeks after the posting due date. Link what you see to specific facts and theories that we have learned about.

You will be assessed on your group participation and discussion responses by the attached rubric.

Map | Sat | Ter | Earth

Mori Point

©2013 Google - Imagery ©2013 Data CSUMB SFML, CA OPC

Our first field trip is planned for Mori Point ⬀

Sign-up for your group *before* joining us on the field trip if you haven't already. Use the course Calendar for scheduled locations and times.

Reply

Figure 4.7 The third iteration requires that the groups' field trip findings be posted to a discussion forum where the entire class can engage in discussion. Note that this iteration also added hyperlinks and embedded a Google Map of the field trip location

- Progressive iterations can lead to more efficient or effective teaching and learning.

For example, you discover in as early as the second or third week of your blended course that students seem unprepared for onsite activities that require them to have studied online materials. You may change that lesson to include a pre-class, online quiz that requires students to have studied the materials.

After you have implemented the pre-quiz into the next unit, you can evaluate student preparation for onsite activities relative to the first unit's iteration. This evaluation can confirm or refute the design decision that you made, which can support the next iteration.

If the change is effective, you would implement the online pre-quiz into all your lesson plans from thereon out. Every such change that you can implement early on means significantly fewer changes later on, after the course design is deemed "complete." Teachers who consistently evaluate and revise in this way can make the iterative development process almost automatic.

Revising is more than simply fixing the prototype and moving on. The goal of revising is to both **improve the existing version** *and* **adapt the results to future lessons**. Thus, the current lesson's latest iteration can serve as a model for the next lesson, which, in turn, is treated as a prototype to be implemented, evaluated, and iterated.

This strategy not only improves the course, lesson by lesson, but it also helps you improve your own design and development skill with each iteration. You'll learn more about effective blended design as you go, and immediately apply that learning to your course.

When you begin designing the subsequent lesson, you'll begin writing outcomes with added experience of seeing the previous unit's outcomes realized through assessments and activities. You improve your writing of outcomes not just by writing more outcomes, but also by seeing them come to life through assessments and activities. Thus, if you prototype a full lesson, writing outcomes for the next lesson will build upon the full design process, and the benefits to your outcome writing skill compound, too.

Iterative development is realized as the benefits of a single revision are compounded throughout the course design.

☑ Plan to improve your course design in small ways, whenever you touch the course.

☑ Evaluations of the course design lead to revisions in future iterations.

4.3 Summary and Standards

> The real test of blended learning is the effective integration of the two main components (face-to-face and Internet technology) such that we are not just adding on to the existing dominant approach or method.
>
> Garrison and Kanuka (2004, p. 97)

Because a blended course introduces so many variables from mixing the onsite and online environments, and because designing and teaching a blended course design is new to many teachers, a simple process can lead to efficient and consistent results.

We recommend a "backward" design process that is learning-centered, starting with learning outcomes before designing assessments that measure those outcomes, and finally creating activities that foster learning. We encourage teachers to focus on a small chunk of the blended course at a time (e.g. a single lesson or unit). This makes iterative development easy—a process of producing a prototype that is meant to be revised in an ongoing fashion based on learning-centered evaluations.

☐ A blended course is the same amount of work as online or onsite versions.

☐ Online or onsite modes are chosen by how their qualities best support learning activities and outcomes.

☐ Resources and activities support learning outcomes.

☐ Assessments determine the degree to which learners have achieved the required learning outcomes.

☐ Plan to improve your course design in small ways, whenever you touch the course.

☐ Evaluations of the course design lead to revisions in future iterations.

References and Further Reading

Anderson, T. (2008). Towards a theory of online learning. In T. Anderson (Ed.), *The theory and practice of online learning* (2nd ed., pp. 45–74). Edmonton, Canada: Athabasca University Press.

Briskman, L. (1980). Creative product and creative process in science and art. *Inquiry*, 23(1), 83–106.

Cohen, A. (1987). Instructional alignment: Searching for a magic bullet. *Educational Researcher*, 16(8), 16–20.

Garrison, D., & Kanuka, H. (2004). Blended learning: Uncovering its transformative potential in higher education. *The Internet and Higher Education*, 7(2), 95–105. doi:10.1016/j.iheduc.2004.02.001.

Graham, C. R., & Robison, R. (2007). Realizing the transformational potential of blended learning: Comparing cases of transforming blends and enhancing blends in higher education. In A. G. Picciano & C. D. Dziuban (Eds.), *Blended learning: Research perspectives* (pp. 83–110). Needham, MA: The Sloan Consortium.

McGee, P., & Reis, A. (2012). Blended course design: A synthesis of best practices. *Journal of Asynchronous Learning Networks*, 16(4), 7–22.

Rathbun, G. A., Saito, R. S., & Goodrum, D. A. (1997). Reconceiving ISD: Three perspectives on rapid prototyping as a paradigm shift. *Proceedings the 1997 National Convention of the Association for Educational Communications and Technology* (pp. 291–296). Albuquerque, NM.

Sims, R., Dobbs, G., & Hand, T. (2002). Enhancing quality in online learning: Scaffolding planning and design through proactive evaluation. *Learning*, 23(2). doi:10.1080/0158791.

Wiggins, G., & McTighe, J. (2005). *Understanding by design* (2nd ed.). Upper Saddle River, NJ: Prentice Hall.

Chapter 5

Planning Your Course from Goals and Outcomes

It's sometimes easy to forget the fundamental questions that drive teachers to teach and students to take a course:

- How will the learner change during the course?
- What is worth learning?
- How can we spend our limited time most wisely?

These questions lead us to define broad course goals and specific learning outcomes that must be paced to fit within the timeline of the semester. Blended courses are no different. In fact, blended courses should have the same goals and outcomes as a face-to-face or online course; it is only the tools and methods that change.

 We introduced a course design map template in Chapter 4. Visit the website to download a copy.

This chapter helps you create **a course design map** that:

- provides a **blueprint** to guide the development of each lesson or unit;
- helps **align assessments and activities** regardless of the technology used to facilitate them;
- encourages **more creative and effective blends** of onsite and online activities.

 ## To Do

By the end of this chapter, your course design map should include a brief description of the course along with a listing of the course's broad goals, organized into lessons or units. You will then select one of those lessons to design as a prototype, and write the specific learning outcomes that relate to the lesson goal(s).

The course design map will also serve as a framework for the course syllabus by providing:

- a concise description of the course;
- a list of broad goals;
- a set of specific learning outcomes related to each goal.

5.1 A Concise Course Description

As a series of learning experiences your course ultimately aims to transform the learners in some ways. We recommend that you **write a concise description of the course** and the impact it will have on target learners. You may already have a course description in your school's course catalog or course syllabus. Now is a good time to review any pre-existing description of the course, and either use it wholesale or edit it to suit the aims of the course.

A course description can be organized around the following:

- **Describe the audience.** Who are the intended learners? What skills do or should they already possess?
- **Summarize the course goals.** What knowledge, skills, or attitudes will the learners have upon successful completion of the course? What topics will be covered?
- **Suggest any strategies you will use**. Generally speaking, how will you teach? How should students learn? This depends on your teaching philosophy and institutional practice, and may develop and change as you design the course.

For example, the course description for "Introduction to Oceanography" states:

> Learners with a basic knowledge of biology and chemistry will develop an understanding of the physical processes influencing oceans and coastal regions, and apply fundamental scientific procedures to questions about the world's oceans. Learners will be able to relate and analyze current understandings of oceanic environmental issues to their own lives.
>
> Learning will happen through direct instruction, hands-on labs, practice activities, field trips, and discussion both within and beyond the classroom walls.

A concise course description identifies the learner audience, course goals, and instructional strategy.

5.2 Mapping Course Goals

The course description suggests what the course is about, generally speaking. The description can be expanded into individual course goals, which describe the learner at the end of the course at a high level.

Goals versus Outcomes

When referring to what learners strive to achieve, there are several sometimes confusing terms that are used by educators (e.g. "standard," "goal," "outcome," "objective"). "Outcome" is perhaps the most commonly used term, and is sometimes used in conjunction with "program-level," "course-level," and "unit-level." We clarify the important distinction between the broad and the specific by using "goals" and "outcomes" to refer to different, but related, descriptions of desired learner performance within a course.

Most courses set high-level *goals* that they want students to achieve. A course goal is too general to be easily measured, so each goal must be elaborated into a set of specific learning *outcomes*. Outcomes detail the knowledge, attitudes, behaviors, and skills that you want learners to develop.

For example, an introductory course on oceanography may break the following goals: ...

Goal 1. Understand theories of the origin of the earth, its atmosphere, and oceans.

Goal 2. Describe the historical development of ocean knowledge.

Goal 3. Understand plate tectonics and its relationship to the formation of major features of the seafloor.

... into more specific learning outcomes, as follows:

Goal 1. Understand theories of the origin of the earth, its atmosphere, and oceans.

1. Describe the development of our earth, atmosphere, and oceans in the context of the solar system and universe.
2. State the basic outline of the geologic column or time scale from 4.6 billion years ago to today.
3. Explain radiometric dating and geo time scale.
4. Contrast absolute and relative dating.

Goal 2. Describe the historical development of ocean knowledge.

1. Describe the diversity of sciences collected to form "oceanography."
2. Summarize the development of oceanography as a science.
3. Explain the significance of navigation in describing oceans and making maps.
4. Recognize different types of maps and charts.
5. Use latitude, longitude, and time to provide navigation with maps and charts.

... and so on.

Reflection

What does a successful student in your course look like when the course is over? What does she know? What does she care about? How does she behave? What can she perform? To what level? In what situations?

Take some time to write down a description of your students before and after they finish the course. Also imagine how their experience in your course affects them five years from now. This kind of visualization can guide you during the blended design process toward engaging students' hearts and minds, and in providing activities and feedback that address their needs.

Each time you finish teaching your blended course, the assessments that you've used should provide a clear picture of each student and how well she matches this vision. If that's not the case, perhaps your assessments aren't measuring the right things!

Where Do Course Goals Come From?

Most teachers will have access to curricula from their school or department that provide course goals. Some schools may have goals stored and available digitally—perhaps through a Learning Management System (LMS). You can save yourself a lot of time, and ensure that you are addressing institutional aims, by finding out if the course goals are available in this way.

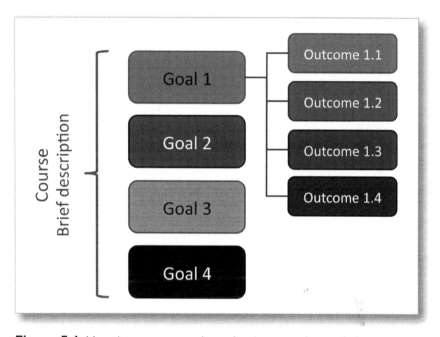

Figure 5.1 Mapping course goals and outcomes shows their relationship and helps focus other course design activities on desired learning

The first goal, "Understand theories of the origin of the earth, its atmosphere, and oceans," describes a general ability or attribute (understanding) that we hope learners will develop during the course. Understanding, however, is difficult to measure. What does understanding mean? What specific theories should learners know about at this stage? How detailed should that knowledge be? How can this be measured?

Breaking a goal down into specific learning outcomes does three things:

1. Describes exactly what is needed to attain the goal.
2. Focuses assessment on evidence of outcomes.
3. Helps teachers pace learning evenly and progressively throughout the weeks of the semester.

 Course goals are clearly written and broadly describe the successful learner at the end of the course.

5.3 Writing Specific Learning Outcomes

Just as the brief course description expands into course goals, course goals each expand into specific learning outcomes—as many as necessary to prove attainment of the goal.

You could go through the entire course and write out the learning outcomes that each course goal branches into, but to get started you really just need to choose one lesson.

Let's return to an example from the "Introduction to Oceanography" course to see how learning outcomes are far more specific than the goal:

Goal 1. Understand theories of the origin of the earth, its atmosphere, and oceans.

Learners will be able to:

1. Describe the development of our earth, atmosphere, and oceans in the context of the solar system and universe.
2. State the basic outline of the geologic column or time scale from 4.6 billion years ago to today.
3. Explain radiometric dating and geo time scale.
4. Contrast absolute and relative dating.

A learning outcome is typically written as *verb* + *object*, where the verb identifies the kind of behavior or skill expected of a proficient learner (e.g. "Explain ...") and the object is the specific task or knowledge (e.g. "... radiometric dating and geo time scale").

The subject of the outcome is implied—it's the learner! But it may be helpful to precede your list of learning outcomes with the phrase, "Learners will be able to ..." This is important to

---

Tip

One way to ensure that your outcomes are clear, concrete, and representative of the kinds of learning you want students to achieve is by basing them on a taxonomy, or set of categories. See Appendix 2 for more details, including a diagram of Bloom's Taxonomy of the cognitive domain and useful verbs that help you write outcomes.

---

remember, because focusing on the learner ensures that we are attending to learning by way of teaching, and not teaching as an end itself.

Learning outcomes should be written explicitly enough that simply reading the outcome lets us easily understand the kind

Outcomes for the Mind and Heart

At the core, instruction involves choosing activities that will engage the learner in achieving the desired learning outcomes. Desired outcomes can be both cognitive (mind) and affective (heart).

Cognitive Outcomes

Related to the mind, these are outcomes that have to do with **knowledge and skills** that the learner acquires. These outcomes are typically measured by having students demonstrate what they *know* and can *do*.

Example: Ability to use a spreadsheet to track the financial balance sheets for a small company.

Affective Outcomes

Related to the heart, these are outcomes that have to do with attitudes or dispositions that suggest **who the learner is becoming**. Typically, these outcomes are much more difficult to measure because they have to do with internal desires.

Example: Commitment to being an accountant who acts honestly and is unwilling to engage in unethical negotiations with clients.

or

Example: Expresses dedication to the health and stability of the oceans through first-hand experiences engaging with the natural world.

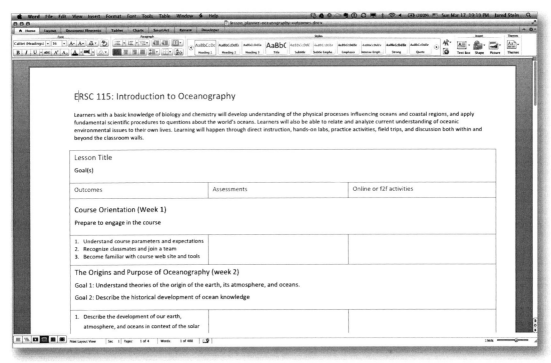

Figure 5.2 Outcomes can be mapped to goals using simple tools like a word processor

Online versus Onsite Learning Time

Set a general framework for your blended course by describing available learning time, as explained in Chapter 1. Understand how much learning time will happen onsite so you can recognize how much can happen online.

Online technology widens the range of kinds of "homework" and other learning activities that can happen outside of class. This is one reason why calculating total learning time is so important when designing a blended course: Online activities can replace both onsite activities *and* traditional activities typically done by students outside of class or in isolation.

of evidence learners could produce to prove their success. A well-written outcome should be clearly measurable, but also allows for a variety of assessment methods.

Learning outcomes should be as succinct as possible. As you write learning outcomes, watch for related outcomes that might be combined without losing specificity. Combining outcomes can be done by understanding how lower-level cognitive skills (such as knowing and understanding) are, in fact, foundational for the higher-level cognitive skills (such as applying and evaluating). See Appendix 2 for an explanation of foundational cognitive skills.

☑ **Learning outcomes for a blended course are identical to those of onsite or online versions.**

☑ **Learning outcomes are measurable and specific.**

☑ **Learning outcomes relate to course goals and are learner-focused.**

5.4 Fitting Goals and Outcomes into a Timeline

Once you have listed all goals, the next step is to **determine how these will fit into the timeline of the course**. For example, if you have five broad course goals, will those each take three weeks of a fifteen-week semester? Some goals may take more time and practice to achieve than others just as some goals will be composed of more outcomes than others.

Goals and outcomes can be organized by lessons to help you map the framework of your blended course. Lessons are discrete chunks of learning activities and assessments that will guide the rhythm of your blended course day-to-day or week-to-week. A lesson may have one or two goals, but rarely more than that. Sometimes a goal is so large that it is stretched across two or more lessons.

Consider the schedule of onsite sessions as you organize lessons. For instance, if your blended course consists of one onsite meeting a week, you might organize lessons around that onsite meeting. Perhaps the onsite session begins or wraps up a lesson. This would imply that a lesson lasts one week.

Then, focusing on one lesson at a time, the goals can be expanded one at a time to list more specific learning outcomes (Table 5.1).

Tip

There is no single method to determine how many goals should be aimed for in a course, but experience suggests that a forty-five-hour course (i.o. three credits) can often be summed up in five or six broad goals.

Table 5.1 An example lesson plan, with one good and several outcomes followed by assessments and activities

Lesson: Intro to Plate Tectonics (week 3)		
Goal: Understand plate tectonics and its relationship to the formation of major features of the seafloor		
Outcomes	Assessments	Online or f2f activities
1. Name the plates and boundaries that make up the surface of the earth's crust. 2. Sketch and describe the interior layers of the earth. 3. Describe the theory of "continental drift." 4. Analyze evidence of seafloor spreading, including hot spots. 5. Apply the theory of seafloor spreading to explain different seafloor sediment thicknesses and ages.	1. 90 percent on practice quiz (many attempts; all outcomes). 2. Participation in onsite peer instruction (SRS data; various outcomes). 3. Concept map assignment (outcomes 1, 2, 3).	1. Watch video lectures and BBC clip (online). 2. Take practice quiz as many times as necessary (online). 3. Concept map walkthrough (face to face & online). 4. Participate in peer instruction activity (face to face). 5. Construct concept map 6. Participate in field trip 1 with team (face to face)

To maximize efficiency, try to design activities and assessments that help students meet multiple outcomes. This is especially applicable when one activity builds on learning from previous activities.

Breaking goals into specific learning outcomes will help you plan for blended assessments (see Chapter 6), as well as the best learning activities that will lead students to those outcomes (Chapters 7 and 8).

In examining how course outcomes fit into the timeline of your course, you may find that goals or outcomes need to be revised, or split, or condensed. *This is a good thing.* Course design improves through iterations, so make a habit of revising at every opportunity (see Chapter 9). In this sense, you can increase clarity and ensure appropriate coverage of topics.

 Sufficient time is allotted for attainment of each learning outcome.

5.5   Planting Goals and Outcomes in Your Course Website

Whether you plan to use an LMS or an independent website as the online hub of your blended course, you can begin seeding the new environment with your goals and outcomes as you write them. Once planted in the course website, the goals and outcomes can easily be linked to assessments and activities down the road, "growing" the outcomes into a full blended learning experience.

An online list of goals and outcomes can also serve as a curriculum map that describes the scope of the course to learners, teachers, and administrators.

If You're Using an LMS ...

Take advantage of LMS tools that allow you to compose and organize outcomes at the course or even department level.

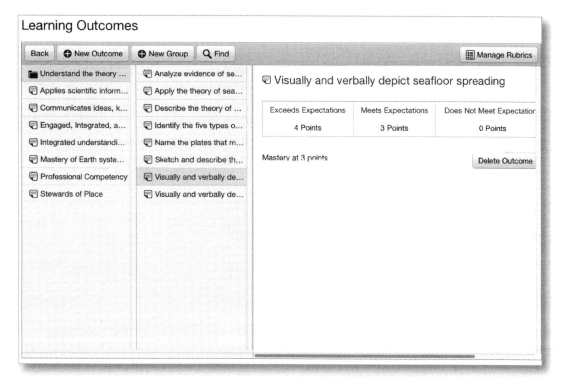

Figure 5.3 LMSs often provide tools for teachers (or, even better, academic departments) to create, organize, and share goals and learning outcomes

Sharing outcomes at the department level means that many teachers can access and use the same outcomes in their courses. Specific learning outcomes may be tied to more general course goals through the use of organizational groups or direct linking.

Consult your campus faculty technology center or LMS documentation to discover how LMS assessments, rubrics, question banks, and activities can be tied to these outcomes. Also, find out what kind of automated reporting or analytics are available for outcome-based assessments through the LMS.

If You're Building Your Own Website ...

Compose a single page that serves as an index for all the goals and outcomes of the course. As you build the course website, you can use simple hyperlinks to point to this index page and even to individually "anchored" learning outcomes.

5.6   Summary and Standards

Setting up a course design map will make the development of your blended course easier and more consistent from start to finish. Starting a brief course description to a set of broad course goals sets the groundwork for elaborating on each goal as a set of specific learning outcomes. Broad course goals relate to specific learning outcomes that are measurable and clearly written.

 Refer to examples of course design maps on the website as you develop your own map.

Specifying goals and learning outcomes is a critical step in blended course design because it helps establish a learning framework for your course design map. Focusing on goals and outcomes will also help ensure your selection of online or onsite activities is learning-focused, not technology-focused. This is why learning outcomes for a blended course should be identical to outcomes for onsite or online versions of the course.

Once you've begun your course design map with a general description and broad course goals, you'll want to choose one lesson to write specific learning outcomes for. You'll develop a prototype lesson as you begin designing assessments and activities that represent attainment of those outcomes.

☐ A concise course description identifies the learner audience, course goals, and instructional strategy.

☐ Course goals are clearly written and broadly describe the successful learner at the end of the course.

☐ Sufficient time is allotted for attainment of each learning outcome.

☐ Plan to improve or iterate your course design in small ways, whenever you touch the course.

☐ Learning outcomes for a blended course are identical to those of onsite or online versions.

☐ Learning outcomes are measurable and specific.

☐ Learning outcomes relate to goals and are learner-focused.

References and Further Reading

Berliner, D. (1990). What's all the fuss about instructional time? In *The nature of time in schools: Theoretical concepts, practitioner perceptions* (pp. 3–35). New York and London: Teachers College Press.

Fink, D. L. (2003). *Creating significant learning experiences: An integrated approach to designing college courses*. San Francisco, CA: Jossey-Bass.

Heer, R. A model of learning objectives—based on *A taxonomy for learning, teaching, and assessing: A revision of Bloom's Taxonomy of educational objectives*. Center for Excellence in Learning and Teaching, Iowa State University. Retrieved from www.celt.iastate.edu/teaching/RevisedBlooms1.html, June 22, 2012.

Krathwohl, D. R. (2002). A revision of Bloom's taxonomy: An overview. *Theory into Practice*, 41(4), 212–218.

Skibba, K. A. (2006). A cross-case analysis of how faculty connect learning in a hybrid course. In *Proceedings of 47th Annual Adult Education Research Conference* (pp. 346–352).

Willingham, D. T. (2009). *Why don't students like school? A cognitive scientist answers questions about how the mind works and what it means for your classroom*. San Francisco, CA: Jossey-Bass.

Chapter 6

Blending Assessment and Feedback for Learning

> The only way we can properly judge where we are is relative to where we want to be.
>
> Wiggins (1998)

Assessments in Blended Environments

Assessments aim to evaluate student attainment of learning outcomes by examining student performance either directly (e.g. by observation) or indirectly (e.g. by an exam). Assessments—and the outcomes they are based on—should reflect the kind of real-world activities or skills that you envision students performing in the future, after they've left your course and are applying what they've learned.

Blended courses can expand the means and methods by which teachers measure student learning by using both onsite and online assessments. This allows teachers to select assessments that are most appropriate for their specific learning outcomes. Onsite, teachers can carefully monitor exams and directly observe presentations, demonstrations, or communication. Online, student work can be submitted and reviewed digitally. Performances can be recorded or live-streamed, knowledge can be objectively assessed through computer-based testing, and progress can be tracked over time through logs, blogs, and analytics.

Assessments don't just measure; they can also provide students with useful feedback. Feedback should happen as soon as possible in order to help students apply it to improve learning. Online tools can automate the delivery of feedback (e.g., through a computerized quiz) and facilitate human interaction around learning experiences (e.g., through an online discussion) with all the flexibility of asynchronous communication. Regardless, teachers can help students mentally prepare to apply feedback by clearly stating when and how they will receive it.

To Do

By the end of this chapter, you will have made notes about specific assessment(s) for a single prototype lesson in your course design map. Your notes should indicate if these assessments take place online or onsite, and what you will need to do to build them. See Table 5.1 in Chapter 5.

Onsite assessments and face-to-face feedback have advantages as well—especially when feedback needs to be delivered with empathy and encouragement. Thus, in a blended course, online and onsite assessments should be interwoven. Blending assessments creates the opportunity to:

- **Improve the variety of assessments.** Students can get maxed out if the same form of assessment is used repetitively. Blended courses increase the range of things that can be done online or onsite: demonstrations, personal communication, research papers, presentations, digital storytelling, automated quizzes, etc. Variety in assessment can ensure that learning outcomes are thoroughly assessed from different angles.

- **Increase the frequency of assessments.** Frequency provides more checks on student progress that tie in to specific outcomes. Frequency can also lower pressure and anxiety by spreading assessments more evenly through the semester. More frequent, lower-stakes assessments are feasible when online tools facilitate management and automated feedback.

- **Focus on authentic assessments.** Authentic assessments aim to be as "real world" as possible, using real-world content or simulative activities. Sometimes these are best done onsite, but online technology makes a lot of things possible that may have been too difficult before, such as sharing digital content from the open Web, and enabling the kind of authentic assessments that might otherwise be too constrained by time and place.

Tip
Assessments don't just provide feedback for students. Teachers can revise future activities and adjust their own instructional practices based on the results of assessments.

- **Enhance feedback on performance.** Feedback is key to helping students understand where they stand. The best feedback will clearly identify what learning outcomes students have not mastered, and how they can improve their performance. But it is a challenge to provide sufficient feedback to all students as frequently as they need it. Online tools can facilitate faster feedback (as some of it can be automated) with greater detail.

☑ Assessments determine the degree to which learners have achieved the required learning outcomes.

☑ Graded assignments are varied (e.g. special projects, reflective assignments, research papers, case studies, presentations, group work, etc.).

☑ Teacher feedback is provided in a timely fashion.

☑ Students know when and how they will receive feedback from teachers.

Reflection

Before you begin exploring blended assessments, think back on your own academic career. Remember the tests, papers, projects, and so on that you had to complete in order to pass classes. Do any of those assessments stand out in your memory? If so, why?

Think of one assessment that seemed quite brilliant at measuring what you actually knew. Now, think of one that did a poor job. What made the difference?

Think of one assessment that guided you to correct any misunderstandings, and led you to learn more and perform better in the future. Also, think of assessments that gave you little or no useful feedback, and if that wasted an opportunity for learning.

Finally, consider if these assessments benefitted from onsite presence or face-to-face interaction. Did they or could they have benefitted from the computer's power of automation, access to information, and instant feedback?

This reflection should prepare you to consider the variety of blended assessment options with effectiveness and personal impact in mind.

New information, including teacher feedback, is followed by opportunities for students to apply the information.

6.2 Onsite Assessments

Designing assessments for a blended course means examining the learning outcomes, coming up with some assessment ideas, and then deciding onsite or online?

Because our onsite time is typically more limited than online time in a blended course, let's begin by looking at specific advantages of the onsite environment for assessment.

Preserving Assessment Integrity

Perhaps the most obvious benefit of conducting assessments onsite is the ease with which teachers can support the integrity of the assessment by directly monitoring students. Even a large room of students can be observed rather efficiently to inhibit, if not fully prevent, cheating. This is an important factor in high-stakes assessments.

This doesn't mean that online assessments are unreliable. Special precautions and design considerations can ensure academic integrity. We share ideas on this topic later in this chapter.

Physical Demonstrations

Assessments of physical activities, whether those are related to sports, crafts, patient interactions, or lab procedures, may be easier onsite. Being physically present with a student during such a demonstration means the teacher can engage multiple senses and observe the student at different angles. They can also provide intervention when needed since the demonstration occurs in real time.

While physical demonstrations can be done online using video recording or conferencing tools, this usually adds an additional layer of complexity and the possibility for technical hiccups that can interfere with the accuracy of the assessment.

Live Presentations

The immediacy and physical presence of the onsite experience also supports assessment of student presentations, speeches, etc. Live presentations are replete with (often unpredictable) distractions and environmental variables that may represent the kind of experiences students may experience in the real world. This provides a degree of authenticity that is especially useful in communication and public speaking courses, for example.

Classroom-based presentations can present two additional authentic learning opportunities:

- Student presenters are subject to the pressure of performing before a real audience.
- Other students form an audience that can engage all their senses to observe, critique, and learn from the presenters.

Note
Certain professions will require online presentation skills. Courses related to sales, marketing, and freelance trades, for example, can provide opportunities for students to practice and be assessed through both live, onsite presentations and online presentations.

Interpersonal Interactions

Language courses often aim to prepare students to communicate with native speakers in varied and sometimes unpredictable scenarios. Language is not just about grammar and vocabulary; language speakers must often include expressions and nonverbal communication to be most effective. Live, in-class assessments of interpersonal interactions challenge students to perform in authentic scenarios.

But the technology barrier is lowering. Advances in both synchronous and asynchronous online video mean that assessing interpersonal interactions is increasingly feasible for anyone. Some LMSs have built these tools in.

 Onsite assessments capitalize on physical presence, immediacy, and human interaction.

6.3 Online Assessments

Because onsite assessments are only necessary in select circumstances, you can think creatively about moving many other kinds of assessments online. The main advantages of online assessment tools are:

- reusability;
- automation;
- multimedia;
- flexibility of time and space.

Reusability and automation in online tools are especially important as they help teachers increase the variety, frequency, and feedback that support learning.

Online Quizzes and Exams

Online quizzing tools can be used to organize and deliver both objective questions (e.g. multiple-choice, matching, fill-in-the-blank) and subjective questions (e.g. essay). There are three key values of online quizzing:

Tip
Time limits on each quiz attempt can be set to encourage students to prepare ahead of time.

- Objective questions can be automatically scored by the computer.
- Specific feedback can be automatically delivered based on students' responses.
- Question selection can be individualized for each student.

These values can save the teacher from the repetitive, time-consuming work of managing, distributing, and correcting quizzes or exams. Online quiz tools also open the door for the use of "quizzing" throughout the course, for practice and repeated drilling. Research on such "retrieval practice" suggests it is an effective tool to promote learning, especially when directly following learning activities.

 See the website for an explanation of how LMS quiz questions can be randomized from various question banks.

Online quizzes can deliver pre-written feedback on any single question or answer choice:

- **Feedback on incorrect answers** can either directly clarify the information or point students back to learning material that explains missed concepts.
- **Feedback on correct answers** can be more than praise or a restatement of the answer. It can elaborate or connect the concept to future learning.

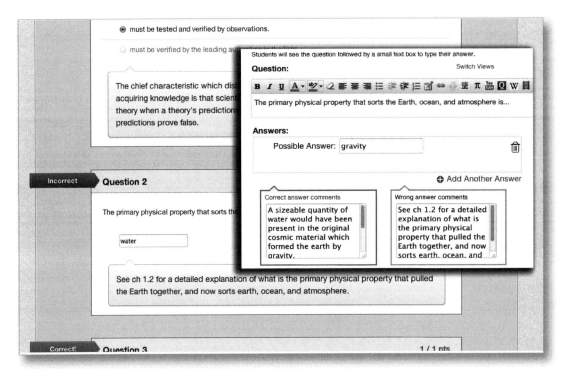

Figure 6.1 This short-answer quiz question has elaborative feedback for a correct response, and corrective feedback for a wrong response

Self-correcting quizzes may allow for multiple attempts, providing students with a chance to apply the automated feedback, go back to lesson materials, and take the quiz again. This encourages students to master material before simply moving on. This also reduces the pressure of high-stakes assessments that may encourage cheating. See Chapter 7 for a detailed look at using online quiz tools for self-assessment activities.

☑ Self-correcting and self-assessment activities are used throughout the course to support practice and increase flexibility of pacing.

☑ Automated feedback provides clarification on incorrect answers and elaborates on correct answers.

Teaching American Sign Language with Multimedia Quizzes

Online quizzes need not be limited to text. Curt Radford of Utah State University uses video "essay" questions in his blended American Sign Language (ASL) course.

Some questions are not questions at all, but rather a video recording of Curt signing a sentence that students must translate from ASL and input a text translation or response. Others are written sentences that students must translate into ASL through a video recording within the quiz interface. Finally, some questions combine both, where Curt signs part of a conversation that students respond to with signs.

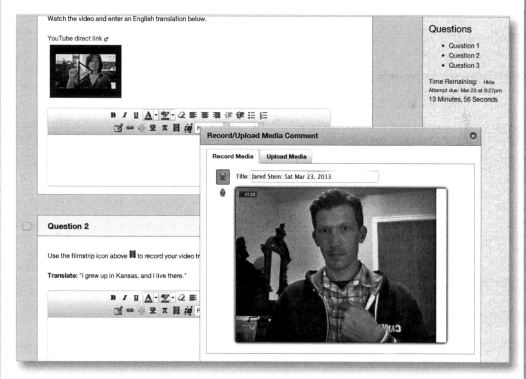

Figure 6.2 When online quizzes allow teachers and students to use video, great things can happen

Because online quizzing tools can often be restricted to time (by date and hour) and space (by a specific computer lab's IP address or by a proctor password), question banks used for quizzes can be repurposed for higher-stakes exams. Informing students that exam questions may come from the same pools of questions that constitute quizzes may encourage students to prepare for and take seriously the formative quizzes.

"Papers" and Projects

The Internet made it immediately obvious that teachers could save a lot of trouble and resources by accepting papers digitally rather than physically. No longer do we have to use paper and toner to print our work. Word processors and office tools allow multiple contributors to comment on, edit, and track changes to a single document.

Accepting online submissions rather than gathering papers in class can save valuable face-to-face time.

Online paper submission can be as simple as sending an attachment through email; however, other online tools allow for greater organization, reliability, and functionality. First, consider something as simple as sharing a document on the cloud, using a service such as Google Docs. Instead of emailing a single, static file, students provide access to a living, changing document that encourages inline commenting and revision. This approach can be used to emphasize **learning as a process, not a destination**.

Online assignment "drop boxes" such as those found in LMSs can centralize both the assessment description as well as the submission process. Be sure that your assessment descriptions include complete instructions, using text, diagrams, or even video explanations, as well as rubrics or other scoring criteria that express your expectations for performance (Figure 6.3).

- magma
- mid-ridge crust
- volcanic activity

Upload your concept map here as a PDF, DOC/DOCX, JPG, or other compatible file type.

File Upload | Website URL

Upload a file, or choose a file you've already uploaded.

File: [Choose File] bern – Seaflo...ept Map.docx

➕ Add Another File

This was my first time trying a concept map. I hope everything is as you expected!

[Submit Assignment] Cancel

Concept Map Rubric

Criteria	Ratings			Pts
A node is provided for for each term	All nodes present 3 pts	Most nodes present 2 pts	Critical nodes missing 1 pts	3 pts
Connectors appropriately link related nodes view longer description	Full array of connectors show relationships 3 pts	Missing a few connecions 2 pts	Missing significant connections 1 pts	3 pts
Connector labels are accurate and descriptive	All connectors labeled appropriately 3 pts	Some missing or inaccurate labels 2 pts	Critical labels missing 1 pts	3 pts
▦ Represents an integrated understanding of Earth geology view longer description threshold: 3 pts	Exceeds Expectations 5 pts	Meets Expectations 3 pts	Does Not Meet Expectations 0 pts	5 pts
			Total Points: 14	

Figure 6.3 This online assignment provides students with instructions, an example, a rubric, and a space to submit their work all in one page

Tip

Cloud-based services such as Google Docs (docs.google.com) and Crocodoc (crocodoc.com) let users share and collaboratively annotate documents online. They also make it easy for teachers to see the development of the document through a revision history, which also tracks individual student contributions.

 Visit the website to see a video of how assignment drop boxes work.

These online tools benefit a variety of online project submissions, including presentation slides, spreadsheets, recorded audio or video, websites, etc.

Rubrics: Even Better Online

Rubrics provide a consistent framework for assessment of student work based on a set of specific criteria. A scoring rubric is typically a grid that includes criteria in rows and rating levels in columns. Descriptors of rating levels are often included to make feedback more complete (Table 6.1).

Table 6.1 This discussion rubric organizes ratings and descriptions by outcome or category

Evaluation criteria	Exceeds requirements	Satisfies requirements	Mostly satisfies requirements	Doesn't satisfy requirements
Quality	Contributions to class discussions are relevant, well-written, and constructive.			
	4	3	2	1
Accuracy	Contributions are supported with evidence as appropriate, and apply new information in meaningful ways.			
	4	3	2	1
Engagement	Contributions are made within the timeline for discussion, and include thoughtful responses to classmates' work.			
	4	3	2	1

Clear, direct communication is critical in a blended course, and that is exactly what a rubric does for an assessment. Organizing online assessments to include description, rubric, and submission all in one space makes it easy for students to understand expectations. More importantly, it provides feedback on how students have met those expectations.

WEB More information on rubrics, including examples, is available on the website.

Rubrics can be done on paper, but online rubrics make scoring submissions easier by providing point-and-click interfaces. Feedback is also easier—and faster—as students simply need to log on to see the completed rubric.

☑ Criteria/rubrics clearly inform learners as to how they will be assessed on specific assignments and provide useful feedback.

Peer Assessment

Peer assessment can provide students with faster, more comprehensive feedback on their work without overburdening the teacher. Peer review doesn't have to be the only assessment of student work; it can be in addition to the teacher assessment.

Peer assessment can improve both the author and the reviewer's work. By assessing their peers' work, students can gain critical insight into the grading process, which can lead to a better understanding of learning outcomes that inform improvement of their own performance. Identifying strengths and weaknesses in peers' work can help them recognize similar attributes in their own work.

Tip
Orient students to online peer review during an onsite session. Walk through your own thought process as you assess an example from a previous semester. Give students a chance to ask questions and clarify the process before reconnecting online.

Online, peer review can be facilitated a number of ways:

- **LMS assignment tools** can automatically and randomly redistribute student submissions for peer review, including any associated rubrics.
- **Email** can be used by the teacher to announce peer review pairing or grouping and to share a rubric. Students can use email to exchange files.
- **Cloud document sharing** services, such as Google Docs, make it easy for students to directly invite classmates to review and even edit their document.
- **Videoconferencing tools** can facilitate peer review of live performances or demonstrations.

Tip
Give students a chance to practice peer review with sample assignments from past semesters.

- **Discussion forums** can provide an open, loosely organized space where peer review can happen by prompting students to share their work and respond to others' work.

In order to ensure that students understand the desired learning outcomes for the assessment, teachers should provide rubrics or standards to peer reviewers. These can be the same instruments that you yourself use to assess work.

Example: Essay #1 Peer Review
After submitting your essay (and the due date has past), return to the online assignment to find one of your classmates' essays for you to review. Use the rubric that I've provided and give constructive and encouraging feedback—the kind of feedback you yourself would like to receive!

6.4 Supporting Academic Honesty Online

One common complaint about online courses is that if assessments can be conducted anywhere, how do we know students aren't cheating? While there are a number of technologies that can be used to restrict or monitor student behavior during an online assessment, we recommend first looking at ways the learning design itself can encourage academic honesty.

Employ an automated "originality" check for online paper submissions. There are several online services that provide students (and teachers) with a report describing whether large parts of the paper appear in previously published works. Rather than being simply a punitive mechanism, this technology can be used to help students understand the sometimes slippery slope that is plagiarism.

See the website for a list of tools or sites that help students understand plagiarism.

☑ Feedback from a variety of sources corrects, clarifies, amplifies, and extends learning.

☑ Criteria and procedures for peer review and evaluation are clear.

Review collaborative contributions. Online tools such as wikis and cloud-based word processors (see p. 100) make it easy for students and teachers alike to see who has contributed to the document, when, and in what form. Encourage students to gauge their own contributions by viewing the revision history of such documents. Teachers can also require that students submit their own contributions page from the revision history.

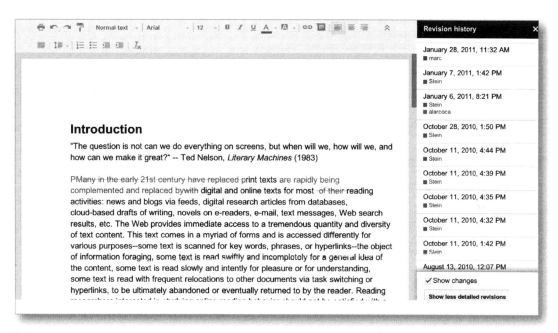

Figure 6.4 Online collaborative document tools such as Google Docs provide a revision history that highlights contributors' work

Assess progressively, in stages. For example, have students submit each phase of a project for assessment, and ensure following phases build on previous work. Early drafts and versions can be submitted for review periodically throughout the semester. This not only discourages cheating, but it also increases the possibility of formative feedback.

A **wiki** is an online website that can be edited by any member of the community—sometimes by anyone at all! Wikipedia.org is currently the world's most famous and successful wiki project.

Reduce the stakes of online quizzing by making the assessments more formative. Allow students to retake the quiz one or more times—this is a standard feature of LMSs.

Make quizzes harder to cheat on by letting the LMS randomize the order and selection of questions and answer choices.

Increase the frequency and variety of assessments throughout the semester to make the mental and physical cost of cheating less rewarding.

Don't eat up students' time with busy work. Courses are designed to fill an average amount of learning time. Giving students too much work—especially "busy work" (which isn't directly tied to learning outcomes or efficient for learning) leaves them less time to prepare for more meaningful assessments. The resulting time crunch may lead some students to cheat.

Make learning meaningful and build intrinsic motivation. Students who are motivated to learn will understand the impact that the learning can have on their lives, and will understand too that the assessments directly tie to that learning. These students will be less inclined to waste opportunities to learn and grow.

Being proactive and conscientiously designing the course to discourage plagiarism is important in a blended course. It is also important that teachers clearly state the consequences of plagiarism, cheating, and failure to properly cite copyrighted materials.

 The consequences of plagiarism, cheating, and failure to properly cite copyrighted materials are emphasized.

ePortfolios

Online portfolios, or eportfolios, are one way of making learning visible. They center on collecting, organizing, and sharing student work with anyone the student chooses: teachers, administrators, family members, employers, prospective grad schools, etc.

ePortfolios are beneficial for assessment because they can express both the breadth and depth of learning. The act of creating an ePortfolio itself can increase learning through reflection and revision—both key components of learning.

ePortfolios in a blended course might be created and collected through an institutional ePortfolio tool. However, you don't need a specific ePortfolio tool to help students curate and share their work. Indeed, if the ePortfolio is truly meant to be representative of the student's work, it should be intentionally owned and controlled by the student. This may mean breaking the ePortfolio space out of institutional control. To this end, it's easy to create websites on your own these days, and blogging platforms have proven to be effective spaces for showcasing one's work.

 See the website for more resources on ePortfolios.

---

ePortfolios as Practice

While ePortfolios do serve as a showcase of work, teachers may be missing an opportunity if they limit the impact of the ePortfolio to a single event: the assessment. Instead, consider ePortfolios as a practice. Just as a resumé must be maintained and updated overtime, so should an ePortfolio grow and develop as the student—the practitioner—grows and develops. Recognizing that ePortfolios are by the student, for the student may be a critical step toward encouraging lifelong learning within and beyond the bounds of the institution.

---

ePortfolios should be assessed with the support of rubrics, with the understanding that outcomes used to construct the rubric should be able to recognize and appropriately measure a broad range of individual student work.

 Course includes ongoing and frequent assessment.

 The size of and due date for graded assignments are reasonable.

6.5 Evidence in the Open

ePortfolios purposely connect various works in an online space as a means of providing a holistic view of the student as a learner. Because it's so easy to create a website these days, simply sharing student work in an ePortfolio is almost trivial. But think beyond the simple one-way transmission of a website and consider other, more social platforms for sharing that will help the student to develop her own online network. Blogs, for instance, provide an online space for individuals to easily create, share, discuss, and revise any kind of digital work on the open Web, for the world to see (Chapter 8).

While not for everyone or every goal, learning and sharing on the open Web can lead to valuable educational outcomes:

- Increased visibility for the student and access to her work.
- Students' digital identities are developed in a proactive, positive way.
- Improved learning based on active practice, diverse feedback, and the positive pressure of publishing.

Project Management for Instructional Designers

Login

▽ **Ch 1: Introduction**
  1.0 Overview
  ⊘ 1.1 Project Management Defined
  ⊘ 1.2 Project Defined
  ⊘ 1.3 Project Context
  ⊘ 1.4 Key Skills of the Project Manager
  ⊘ 1.5 Introduction to the Project Management Knowledge Areas
▷ **Ch 2: Profiling**
▷ **Ch 3: Organization**
▷ **Ch 4: Expectations**
▷ **Ch 5: People**
▷ **Ch 6: Technology and Communication**
▷ **Ch 7: Starting**
▷ **Ch 8: Time**
▷ **Ch 9: Costs**
▷ **Ch 10: Quality**
▷ **Ch 11: Risks**
▷ **Ch 12: Closure**
  About
    Authors
    License

Chapter 1. Introduction to Project Management

Welcome to *Project Management for Instructional Designers*. This book is an adaptation of *Project Management from Simple to Complex* written by Russell Darnall and John Preston and generously published under an open license by Flat World Knowledge. The book you are now reading is a work in progress. If you are interested in contributing to this version of the book, please contact David Wiley at Brigham Young University.

This book provides an overview of project management, defining both projects and project management. Along with information on the essential basics of project management, we have also included videos of experienced instructional designers discussing real life applications of the principles you will be learning.

The content is organized in a roughly chronological pattern, corresponding to the order in which you will likely be called on to use the principles in this book. Thus chapters 2 and 3 explain the pre-project legwork, including how to accurately profile a project and organize the division of labor. The middle chapters discuss such topics as how to understand and meet client expectations, how to successfully work together as part of a team, and how to manage project scheduling, quality, and costs. The final chapter explains the necessary steps in closing out a project once the work has been completed

Figure 6.5 Students in David Wiley's project management course collaborated on a book as the course project. The book is openly licensed and published online.

- Greater motivation to engage in learning and sharing through the rewards and attention of a social community.

If you decide that student engagement with real-world networks on the open Web is important for your course goals, blended courses provide a perfect opportunity to encourage students to share in this way.

6.6 Set Expectations with Clear Instructions

Students will want to plan their performance on a clear understanding of the assessment and its alignment to learning outcomes. Teachers should make the relationship between assessments and outcomes clear so that students are encouraged to track their own progress toward course goals.

Teachers should provide succinct but thorough instructions for the completion of assessments.
Remember, every extra moment that a student spends deciphering instructions is one moment less spent on the actual learning. Thus, instructions must be stated simply, clearly, and logically.

When possible, assessments should be preceded by examples that explain the mechanics of the assessment. Student examples from previous courses—both high- and low-achieving—can help students form mental models of expectations. Teachers can also provide worked examples that

---

Assess Learning, Not How Tech-Savvy the Student Is

Assessment methods should measure the desired learning outcomes, not skill using technology. For instance, a student may be a great presenter, but may have a hard time using online technology to record a presentation. Blended courses should:

- List all necessary technology skills in the course syllabus so students understand what is expected.
- Exercise students' technology skills early by providing simple, ungraded practice assignments that are similar to future assignments.

explain their own expert thought process as they themselves work through the assessment activity. See Chapter 7 for more details on worked examples.

Finally, because students in a blended course expect activity to happen in at least two different spaces—online and onsite— the manner of submission for any graded assignment or assessment must be perfectly clear to eliminate confusion. Presuming that some assessments and activities will be completed online, a blended course should also provide students with access to tutorials or help documentation on using the course website.

- ☑ **Instructions and requirements are stated simply, clearly, and logically.**

- ☑ **The relationship between learning outcomes and assessments is evident.**

- ☑ **Students are given clear expectations and criteria for assignments. Examples are included for clarification when needed.**

- ☑ **The manner of submission for graded assignments is clear.**

6.7 Online Grading

Different online toolsets will provide different tools for assessing student work. Because so much instructional time may be spent on evaluating and scoring assessments, we recommend thoroughly investigating your options, and finding the fastest, most efficient path to providing feedback to your students. Ask your colleagues and campus technologists for methods and tips.

Tip
Don't confuse measuring activity with measuring results.

We explored some ways of facilitating online feedback in this chapter, from automated assessment of objective questions in quizzes to rubric-based teacher and peer assessment of papers and projects. But regardless of the method of feedback, teachers will need a place to store assessment scores so that the relationship between graded elements and the final grade is made clear to students. The grade breakdown may be in the course syllabus, or simply expressed through an online gradebook. Online gradebooks are probably the most often used feature of a LMS—they put the management in Learning Management System.

Online gradebooks may be updated:

- Manually, by typing in scores into gradebook columns.
- Automatically, from objective, online quizzes.
- Semi-automatically, from manually scored online rubrics.
- From spreadsheet upload, if you're keeping scores offline.

Student Name	Secondary ID	Roll Call Atten Out of 100	Introductions Out of 15	Quiz on Lab ...	Read the Sy...	Assignment 1: Out of 14	Assignment 2: ...	Assignment 3...	Multimed Or
Annie Bern Intro to Oceanography -	sdemo+annie@ins...	71%	15	10	✔	12	-	-	
Ada Rabinovich Intro to Oceanography -	mrjstein+ada@gm...	62%	15	9	✔	13	-	-	
Greg Samsa Intro to Oceanography -	mrjstein+gregor@...	97%	9	9	✔	12	-	-	
Test Student Intro to Oceanography -	d6f0a15aec2fa34...	-	💬	-	✘	-	-	-	
William Tangle Intro to Oceanography -	william@tangledro...	100%	💬	10	✔	12	-	-	

Figure 6.6 A simple, online gradebook with scores from several sources

One of the most important features of an online gradebook is its ability to calculate a weighted or customized final percentage or letter grade (see Chapter 9 for a discussion of grading schemes in blended courses). Some gradebooks can even drop the lowest score(s) from a set of assessments.

By itself, an online gradebook can impact student performance by providing a reliable, up-to-date, on-demand calculation of scores. This, of course, depends on the teacher's responsiveness in scoring student work, and on the student checking his grades. Some LMSs also provide automatic alerts to students through email or social media as a means of providing faster feedback and notification, which may reduce that barrier and lead to further engagement.

☑ The relationship between graded elements and the final grade is clear.

☑ Students can easily track their progress.

6.8 Summary and Standards

Assessment is critical to determine the effectiveness of our instruction and the learning activities. Formative assessments provide rich feedback critical to inform students of their own progress and improve learning. Blended courses offer the broadest array of tools yet to assess learning. There is no need to sacrifice the values of face-to-face assessment, and yet one is compelled to take advantage of the many online assessment tools that can provide frequent and diverse assessments throughout the course term (Table 6.2).

Students who create digital works as evidence of learning can collect and showcase these through an ePortfolio, or simply share them on the open Web in their own digital space, such as a blog or personal website. Sharing in the open is one way to link classroom assessments to the real world.

Table 6.2 Advantages of onsite or online assessment types

Type of Assessment	Onsite Advantages	Online Advantages
Quizzes and exams	Easier to control against cheating	Individualized question selection Automated scoring Automatic feedback Multiple attempts
Live presentations and physical demonstrations	Sensory richness Fewer technology barriers	Flexibility of space
Papers and projects	Peer review may benefit from human connection	Digital submission collection Online rubrics Peer review management Gradebook integration
ePortfolios	Allows for physical objects Sensory-richness	Portability Share-ability Publishing in online space

☐ Assessments determine the degree to which learners have achieved the required learning outcomes.

☐ Graded assignments are varied (e.g. special projects, reflective assignments, research papers, case studies, presentations, group work, etc.).

☐ Teacher feedback is provided in a timely fashion.

☐ Students know when and how they will receive feedback from teachers.

☐ New information, including teacher feedback, is followed by opportunities for students to apply the information.

☐ Onsite assessments capitalize on physical presence, immediacy, and human interaction.

☐ Self-correcting and self-assessment activities are used throughout the course to support practice and increase flexibility of pacing.

☐ Automated feedback provides clarification on incorrect answers and elaborates on correct answers.

☐ Criteria/rubrics clearly inform learners as to how they will be assessed on specific assignments and provide useful feedback.

☐ Feedback from a variety of sources corrects, clarifies, amplifies, and extends learning.

☐ Criteria and procedures for peer review and evaluation are clear.

☐ Course includes ongoing and frequent assessment.

☐ The size of and due date for graded assignments are reasonable.

☐ Instructions and requirements are stated simply, clearly, and logically.

☐ The relationship between learning outcomes and assessments is evident.

☐ Students are given clear expectations and criteria for assignments. Examples are included for clarification when needed.

☐ The manner of submission for graded assignments is clear.

☐ The relationship between graded elements and the final grade is clear.

☐ Students can easily track their progress.

References and Further Reading

Amado, M., Ashton, K., Ashton, S., et al. (2011). Project management for instructional designers. Retrieved from http://idpm.us.

Hall, H., & Davison, B. (2007). Social software as support in hybrid learning environments: The value of the blog as a tool for reflective learning and peer support. *Library and Information Science Research*, 29, 163–187.

Hounsell, D. (2003). Student feedback, learning and development. In M. Slowey & D. Watson (Eds.), *Higher education and the lifecourse* (pp. 67–78). Berkshire, UK: Open University Press.

Karpicke, J. D., & Roediger, H. L. (2008). The critical importance of retrieval for learning. *Science*, 319(5865), 966–968.

Lemley, D., Sudweeks, R., Howell, S., et al. (2007). The effects of immediate and delayed feedback on distance learners. *Quarterly Review of Distance Education*, 8(801), 251–260.

Radford, C., & Legler, N. (2012). Exploring the efficacy of online ASL. Conference presentation. InstructureCon 2012, Park City, Utah. Retrieved from http://vimeo.com/45325373.

Sadler, P. M., & Good, E. (2006). The impact of self- and peer-grading on student learning. *Science Education*, 11(1), 1–31.

Shea, P. (2007). Towards a conceptual framework for learning in blended environments. In A. G. Picciano & C. D. Dziuban (Eds.), *Blended learning: Research perspectives* (pp. 19–35). Needham, MA: The Sloan Consortium.

Wiggins, G. (1998). *Educative assessment: Designing assessments to inform and improve student performance*. Hoboken, NJ: Jossey-Bass.

Chapter 7

Blending Content-Driven Learning Activities

The critical factor in blending a course centers on selecting each mode—online or onsite—to take advantage of their strengths and diminish their weaknesses. This is why rethinking everything you do in the traditional face-to-face classroom is critical for a transformative blended course.

While assessments are intended to measure learning and provide feedback on student performance, there are many other learning activities that may not be measured. Many of these are *receptive* activities: reading, viewing a demonstration, and listening to a lecture. Other activities link these knowledge sources to activities that reinforce the information and provide opportunities to practice. Frequent and varied learning activities help learners develop mental models, or *schemata*, which are necessary for expertise.

7.1 Designing Activities for Efficiency and Purpose

Because we have limited learning time in any course, we need to focus learners on the most efficient and engaging learning activities, those that directly prepare them for the assessments that themselves demonstrate the learning outcomes for the course.

Learning activities should continually lead students toward specific outcomes, preparing them to perform on assessments along the way. The backward design model bases learning activities on assessments that are properly aligned with outcomes. With alignment assured, we can then make better decisions about where the activities should take place.

Figure 7.1
Backward design
ensures activities
lead to
assessments and
then outcomes

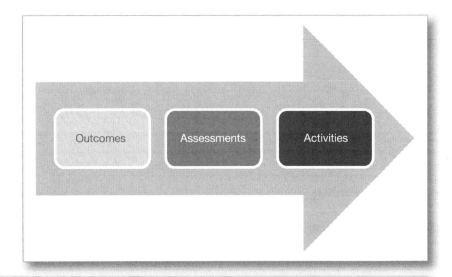

Reflection

Think back on a complex skill that you have learned, or a concept you have
mastered and put into practice. Choose something that you are good at and,
indeed, proud of. How did you learn that skill or concept?

In the case of a skill:

- At what point did you try to do it yourself?
- How authentic or real-world was the situation in which you first tried it?
- How did you determine if you'd done well on that first attempt? How
  important was feedback in helping you try it again and improving?

In the case of knowledge:

- How did you first recognize that you needed to understand this thing?
- How did you begin learning about it? Did you ask an expert? Consult a
  book? Search the Web?
- How did you test the knowledge that began to develop? Did you try to
  apply the information in social situations, with colleagues, or on a project?
- What feedback helped you recognize where your understanding was
  insufficient? How did you know where to go to learn more?

This reflection should help you understand what was personally effective or
ineffective in a learning experience. Remember that no two learners are
exactly alike, and how quickly you are able to learn something depends,
in large part, on your background knowledge.

Resources and activities support learning outcomes.

Onsite or Online?

To Do

As you work through this chapter, continue to use the course design map (see Chapters 4 and 5) as a place to plan and make notes about the kinds of activities that will lead students to perform successfully on assessments, and reach course goals and outcomes.

Think about each of the following learning activities and ask yourself the principal question of blended course design: is this better suited for onsite or online?

Table 7.1 Onsite or online

Learning Activity	Onsite?	Online?
Attending a lecture	☐	☐
Hands-on practice	☐	☐
Quizzes	☐	☐
Discussing topics as a group	☐	☐

Most of these activities can be done onsite or online, but each mode may provide different strengths or weaknesses. For example, some say the lecture is a natural fit for online, as it not only saves the teacher time in the long run, but it also gives students flexibility to watch the lecture on their own time, when they're most ready—and to review it as needed. Others might counter-argue that a great lecture should be face to face, as it incorporates teacher–student interaction—even if that interaction is nonverbal, in the form of facial expressions or gestures. Such interaction can lead the teacher to alter his lecture on the fly, and even change the entire course of the lecture to engage in useful detours or tangents.

Tip
If you are not familiar with a lot of online technologies or tools, start small. Begin blending using the technologies you are most comfortable with, so that your technological literacy supports instruction and doesn't impede learning.

New information is rarely enough by itself. Learners also need frequent opportunities to apply the new information. The nature of a blended course allows for the greatest variety of learning activities, online or onsite. Teachers have the opportunity to ensure frequency and increase the variety as they choose the most effective and efficient activities for the outcomes.

This chapter closely examines *content-driven* learning activities—activities based primarily on new information or material that students must learn and work with. The next chapter focuses on *community-driven* learning activities—activities focused on the kind of social learning that emerges when a community of learners interacts. Both kinds of activities support student engagement, and can be used in concert to downplay weakness of one while amplifying the strengths of another.

 Activities are frequent and varied.

 Activities encourage interactions that involve course content and personal communication.

7.2 Interactive Lectures, Presentations, and Demonstrations

Lectures have a bad reputation. The core function of a lecture is to communicate information to an audience of learners. This may seem too passive to be considered an activity. And while communication of information remains a central teaching activity, traditional onsite lectures are made obsolete by more efficient—and often more effective—transmission through digital text, images, and video.

A better lecture is an *active* experience where students:

- challenge their own assumptions about the topic;
- engage with the teacher and their classmates about the content;
- immediately apply new information.

> ## John Medina's Ten-Minute Lecture
>
> Dr John Medina is a developmental molecular biologist who has won numerous teaching awards. In his book *Brain Rules*, Medina describes a lecture format that has improved student learning and maintained engagement in his university courses:
>
> - **Ten minutes** for each lecture segment, no more.
> - **Present meaning before detail**. Give a one-minute gist to introduce each segment.
> - **Remind learners "where we are"** with each segment, and explain how the current segment relates to the rest of the class session.
> - **"Bait the hook" at the end** of each segment in order to buy yourself another ten minutes. Use emotion and relevance to hook students' interest.

Incorporating these principles results in *interactive lectures*, and these can be accomplished both online or onsite. Interactive lectures combine delivery of new information—the course content—with an application activity.

Presenting Information Effectively

Here are some ways that lectures and presentations can be improved:

- **Break up blocks of information** into incremental "chunks" that are more manageable in memory.
- Center lectures on **questions**, not just telling answers.
- Use **case studies, stories, or anecdotes** to illustrate real-world relevance.
- Include **human elements such as emotion and conflict** to engage the audience.
- Use **animations or video** to help express complex ideas or relationships.
- Have learners **immediately apply new information** through self-test, peer instruction, or class discussion activities.
- Model expert behavior and strategies by **thinking aloud** as you work through a problem or task.

Tip

Students can listen to you speak or read words on screen, but not both at the same time. Avoid presenting text (e.g. a detailed outline of the lecture topic) when lecturing or narrating, as this splits attention and leads to extraneous cognitive load.

Correcting Students' Misunderstandings with Q&A Videos

Figure 7.2 Derek Muller's Veritasium videos come in two parts. The first video prompts students to predict what will happen (www.youtube.com/user/1veritasium)

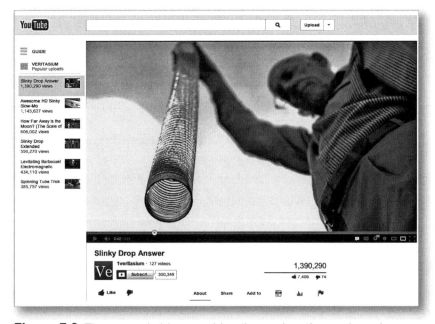

Figure 7.3 The second video provides the explanation and can be preceded or followed with online or onsite activities

Research suggests that **students tend to ignore new information in favor of their own pre-existing understanding**, even if it's wrong. Derek Muller recommends introducing a topic in a video by first illustrating one or more common misunderstandings. Calling attention to misunderstandings will help students adjust their faulty mental models when presented with correct information.

Online Interactive Lectures

What?

A teacher, lecturer, or guest expert is recorded digitally with a microphone or webcam. The resulting media is uploaded to a course Web server. Students access, view, and review these lectures on their own schedule, when they can give their fullest attention.

Lectures become interactive when followed by an application activity. The lecture can also be preceded by activities that prompt students to question their own assumptions and identify problems in their understanding (e.g., see *Synchronous Peer Instruction* in Chapter 8).

Why?

Lectures are perhaps one of the easiest learning activities to convert to online, and offer many benefits in a digital format:

- **Reusability.** Record a series of lectures, and save yourself the time of performing them class after class, semester after semester.
- **Flexibility.** Students can watch lectures when they want. And review them as many times as needed.
- **Portability.** Students can take lectures on their phones or MP3 players, giving them a chance to watch or re-watch.
- **Efficiency.** A carefully scripted lecture will likely be shorter and more concise than one given in the classroom, especially when questions or sidetracks are avoided.

Where?

Students access files through the Learning Management System (LMS), or a streaming media server, or through a social media site such as YouTube or Vimeo.

Students watch or listen to these lectures either on their computer or on a mobile device such as a tablet or phone (Figure 7.4).

Questions and discussions around the video can take place in an online discussion forum, or in follow-up, onsite Q&A.

Who?

Lectures can be delivered by the teacher or a guest expert. The whole class is expected to watch or listen to the lecture, but this is done individually as opposed to *en masse*. This lets students have greater control over the experience.

How?

Digital lectures can be created on most computers simply by using a webcam and microphone. This may be done in your office, at your home, on location, or in a recording studio (many colleges and universities make these spaces available to faculty).

Figure 7.4
Digital videos can be conveniently accessed from mobile phones and other connected devices

Digital lecture files can be uploaded to (or even recorded directly within) an LMS, streaming media server, or social media site such as YouTube or Vimeo.

Online lectures can produce a "feed" that students can subscribe to, ensuring that their device automatically downloads the latest lectures.

Tip

If you demonstrate, ask students to predict what will happen. If their prediction is incorrect, thinking about it ahead of time will make their cognitive dissonance greater and help them adjust their faulty mental model (Rosenberg et al. 2006). This can be done online through discussion forums that hide other responses until a student has himself responded.

☑ Audio and video material appearing within a lesson should be brief.

☑ Blocks of information are broken up into incremental chunks to support memory.

☑ New information is immediately followed by opportunities for students to apply the information.

☑ Stories, anecdotes, emotion, or human conflict are used to engage learners and show real-world relevance when appropriate.

☑ Content is designed to be simple and clear so as to avoid information overload (e.g. avoid narrating while written text is visible, using distracting images for decoration, presenting too much information at once, etc.).

Producing Digital Audio and Video

Creating and sharing digital video has never been easier. Still, it can be a daunting task for those who have little experience or inadequate resources. Here are some tips on creating digital lectures for online delivery:

- **Keep it simple.** Content is more important than production value, so don't be afraid to use whatever video equipment you have—a webcam, a phone camera, etc.
- **Protect students' privacy** if you record lectures live, in a real classroom. Get written permission from students if they will be on camera.
- **Use audio alone when the topic doesn't require visuals.** Audio files provide even more flexibility as students can listen to them while working out or commuting.
- **Use screencasting software for computer-based demonstrations** when you need to show websites or software (Table 7.2). This works for recording slide presentations, too.
- **Use a quality microphone** if you're going to record many lectures. You can also see if your school has microphones to loan.
- **Provide lecture files in standard file formats** to ensure students can access these on a wide variety of devices. For video, aim for MP4/M4V, AVI, or MOV. For audio, use MP3.

A sample student permission form is available on the website.

One of the key advantages of digital video is that students gain the flexibility to watch the video when they want, where they want, and as many times as needed. However, students may also be tempted to multitask, and watch lectures passively or with distractions. The box below shows an example of such guidance that can be included with each online video as a reminder.

Get the Most out of Videos
You'll learn best if you watch class videos:

- only when you can give your full attention;
- in conjunction with related activities (e.g., practice quizzes);
- as many times as needed to review or study.

Tip
Posting videos to social media sites such as YouTube or Vimeo under a **Creative Commons** (CC) license is a great way to share your teaching beyond the limits of the classroom. CC lets you determine how others can reuse your work without having to bother you for permission. See http://creativecommons.org for more information.

☑ Presentations are designed to engage and support learner attention.

☑ Resource material is accessible to all students in commonly used formats.

☑ Pedagogical steps build progressively, one upon the other, as is appropriate to the subject matter.

☑ Non-essential materials that may present extraneous cognitive load are avoided.

Table 7.2 Free software for recording video or screencasts

Software	Description	OS	URL
Jing	Record short screencasts with audio	Win, Mac	techsmith.com/jing.html
CamStudio	Record screencasts with audio and callouts	Win	camstudio.org
Screencast-O-Matic	One-click screen capture recording.	Browser-based, Mac	screencast-o-matic.com
Movie Maker	Record and edit audio and video from your computer	Win	windows.microsoft.com/en-US/windows/get-movie-maker-download
iMovie, Photobooth, QuickTime	Built-in tools to record audio or video on Macs	Mac	N/A

7.3 Worked Examples and Practice Activities

When learning involves developing skill, learners need both new information and the opportunity to apply that information in practice. Blended course designs can take advantage of the reusability of online materials to present new information as worked examples, and leverage onsite meetings to promote efficient practice and corrective feedback.

Worked Examples

What?

A worked example presents a challenge and explains the correct method of working through the challenge each step of the way. The steps build progressively, one upon another (Figures 7.5 and 7.6). After a worked example, students should have opportunities to practice and solve similar problems on their own, with corrective feedback provided as needed.

Why?

Effective instruction of skills often comes in the form of explanation, and worked examples are a proven method of explaining processes. The step-by-step explanation gives learners insight into the expert's process of solving the challenge, eliminating much of the mystery that may impede their progress.

Where?

This is onsite when physical objects are involved or when interpersonal interaction is required. This is online in most other cases.

Who?

The teacher or other expert provides the worked example.

The class as a whole or individually observes and applies the worked example. Learners can themselves create worked examples to explain the process.

How?

Begin by identifying the challenge or concept, then outline the process that an expert would work through, paying attention to thought processes. This outline can be used to construct the worked example as a variety of media. For example:

- A web page with text, images, or diagrams.
- A video as part of a lecture.

For onsite worked examples, the teacher should map out the process himself ahead of time in order to demonstrate and explain.

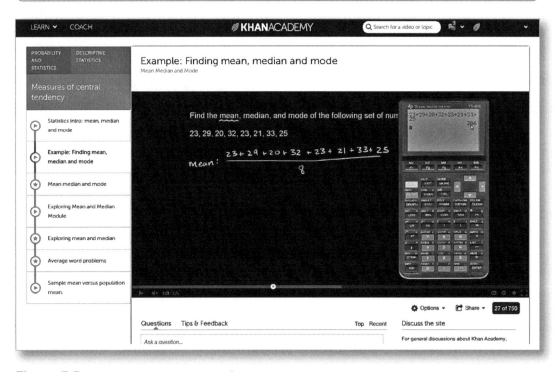

Figure 7.5 This worked example is a video that explains the cognitive processes used to determine the mean, median, and mode of a set of numbers (video from Khan Academy, CC By-NC-SA)

Step 3 - Float and Size the List Items

Let's begin turning this list of shoe images into a gallery by **setting the LIs to float to the left.**

If we don't set a size, each LI will only be as large as its content. **Let's size these to be about a third of the width of the parent (30%)** and add some **margins on the right of each (3%)** so they're not too close together:

```css
.gallery {
   margin: 0;
   padding: 0;
   list-style: none;
}

.gallery li {
   float: left;
   width: 30%;
   margin: 0 3% 0 0;
   padding: 0;
}
```

That's looking good already!

Figure 7.6 This worked example from a blended Web design course uses text and images to walk students through a web page design activity, step by step

"Hands-On" Guided Practice

You can't learn a skill just by watching a video or reading a book—you have to actually attempt the skill yourself. "Hands-on" practice lets learners develop a skill by doing—either on their own or under supervision. Learners' early attempts will

Tip
Deliberately using authentic examples from the open Web can help students eventually transition from teacher-centric classroom learning to independent, lifelong learning.

need guidance until they develop enough capability to practice on their own.

To help students to transfer what they learn to real-world situations, we should design activities that are **authentic**, or as close to real-world experiences as possible. Take advantage of onsite environments when hands-on practice needs to match real-world scenarios and engage multiple senses (e.g. face-to-face interaction with people or hands-on interaction with physical objects). The value of onsite, hands-on practice can be critical in early stages so that the teacher can observe and quickly intervene to correct and scaffold students' efforts.

Tip
Don't distract students with purely supplemental materials. Learning time is limited in any course, and research suggests that non-essential materials can present extraneous cognitive load that may impede student progress toward learning outcomes. Provide supplements in a special section of the course, if at all.

Accessibility and Universal Design

In order to support all students in their learning, regardless of any disabilities they may have, teachers are responsible for providing learning activities in an accessible format. For example, if you provide content in audio format, you must provide a text transcript of the same content for students who may be deaf. A video may require captioning, or a *collated text transcript* that includes descriptions of visuals and actions in addition to spoken words.

Universal design is the label given to media design that takes into account the diversity of accessibility issues that users may face. In essence, universal design aims not at facilitating a single disability, but providing content and activities in a way that is universally accessible for different people and devices.

Many countries have laws that direct or regulate accessibility of state-funded educational experiences (e.g. ADA section 508 in the US), so contact the appropriate office at your institution for guidance.

Sophisticated multimedia learning activities can simulate many real-world scenarios and provide students with opportunities to practice "hands-on" activities, but these are also labor-intensive to create, and require specialized skill with multimedia software.

 See the website for a list of the resources and tools shown in this chapter.

Dynamic Content and Simulations

Most online content is currently static content. The organization and visual design of static content has a significant impact on students' willingness to engage with the content. Imagine a student sitting in front of two online lessons. The first lesson is 95 percent text organized into large blocks while the second is a lesson with smaller blocks of text laced with graphic images and even a short video or two. Which lesson is likely to be more enticing to the student?

Research note: **A prominent distance education researcher, Börje Holmberg, claimed that students would better engage with static content if the content was written in a conversational tone similar to an instructor talking with a student rather than the kind of language typically found in a textbook.**

There is an increasing amount of dynamic content available to supplement the static content available online. Imagine the engagement of a student using a simulation tool such as Google Sky to explore and learn about the planets in the universe (Figure 7.7) or a student using the Virtual ChemLab to see the effects of combining chemicals that would be much too dangerous to handle in a lab setting (Figure 7.8).

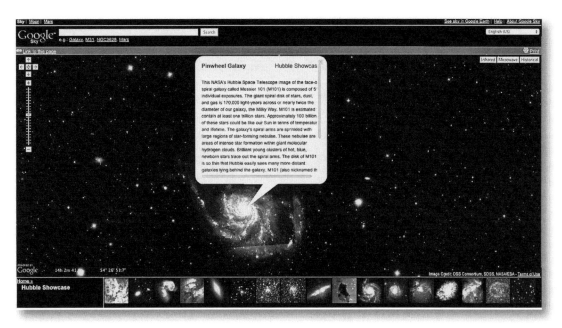

Figure 7.7 Google Sky is a simulated view of the universe based on the best astronomical data (http://google.com/sky)

Figure 7.8 Virtual ChemLab provides realistic simulations of chemistry and other subjects. Brigham Young University and Prentice Hall (http://chemlab.byu.edu/)

Activity: Hands-On Guided Practice in the Computer Lab

When computer skills (e.g. programming or software applications) are part of the learning outcomes, a computer lab can become a powerful space for onsite, hands-on practice.

After studying worked examples, students in a computer lab are given directions from the teacher to accomplish one or more tasks. Students may be assigned partners to help scaffold their efforts, compare results, and guide each other if they get stuck. The teacher moves through the lab, encouraging the class, monitoring individual student performance, and providing individualized instruction and intervention for those who may struggle.

Upon completion of the tasks, students should reflect on their progress, make note of their struggles, and set goals for further practice on their own.

Figure 7.9 Onsite lab experiences can efficiently combine instruction with monitoring and correcting of student performance. Image credits: "Computer Lab" by Saint Louis Madrid Campus, CC By-ND (http://flickr.com/photos/slumadrid campus/6263462648/)

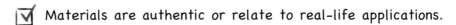 Materials are authentic or relate to real-life applications.

☑ Presentations include examples, models, case studies, illustrations, etc. for clarification.

7.4 Online Self-Assessments

In Chapter 6, we saw how online tools can support formal assessments such as quizzes, exams, and tests. Online quizzes are ideal for practice activities, too, thanks to their ability to randomize questions and provide feedback automatically. Self-assessments can utilize online quiz tools or simply rely on a worksheet with answer key to provide students a chance to test and self-assess their knowledge.

Self-Assessment Quiz

What?
An online quizzing tool delivers questions to students, which may include true/false, multiple-choice, matching, or short-answer. The quiz is automatically scored and provides immediate feedback to the learner (see Chapter 6).

Why?
Self-assessment quizzes are quick, low stakes, and thus low stress. They stimulate recall of important information and challenge students to engage lower-order cognitive skills as a means of ensuring knowledge and understanding.

The results are automatic and immediate, providing actionable feedback to the learner without requiring additional work by the teacher. Repeated attempts can lead to mastery.

Where Does it Happen?
Most LMSs provide a quizzing tool that lets you create questions with automatic feedback, organize question banks, randomly pull questions from larger pools, and set parameters for the quiz. Quizzing tools automatically score and provide feedback.

Who?

Individual students.

How?

Creating the Quiz

LMSs tend to be very good at facilitating online quizzes. Here are some basic steps:

- **Add questions to an online question bank.** Compose your own questions or download questions from publishers or open education resources. Try to find multiple questions for each learning outcome.
- **Craft feedback for correct and incorrect answers.** Feedback on incorrect answers should explain why the answer was wrong and refer learners back to materials for review. Feedback on correct answers should elaborate on the topic.
- **Organize questions.** If possible, have questions organized according to learning outcomes, and randomly select questions for each outcome from larger groups.
- **Set parameters of the quiz.** This may include making sure learners can see appropriate quiz results, allowing for one or multiple attempts, setting a cut-off date, or establishing a time limit.
- **Publish the quiz.** Make the quiz obvious to learners by providing a direct hyperlink to it from the course outline, via the course calendar, or through an announcement.
- **Review results and revise the quiz.** Most LMS quiz tools provide quiz statistics or *item analysis* that can reveal effective or ineffective questions or answer choices.

Taking the Quiz

Students take the quiz and immediately see results. They can review feedback on individual questions, and review materials before reattempting the quiz.

Some quizzes require mastery (e.g. 80 percent) before other materials can be accessed.

> Research note: Actively recalling information is not only more effective than simply reviewing information, but also reflects knowledge gaps, which can direct further study (deWinstanley & Bjork 2002).

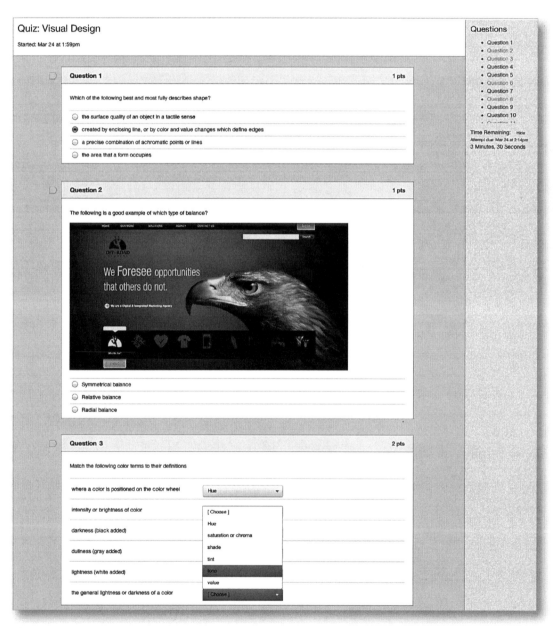

Figure 7.10 The student experience of an online reading quiz with multiple-choice and short-answer questions

Self-assessments happen after or before a presentation or work example:

- After, to provide a chance to immediately apply and reinforce the information.
- Before, to pre-assess understanding and help students self-identify problems.

Activity: Pre-Class Reading Quizzes

Pre-class reading quizzes require students to complete the reading and provide teachers with just-in-time feedback on the class's understanding of key topics.

These quizzes should occur regularly (e.g., preceding each onsite meeting). Follow the same directions for self-assessment quizzes, with the due date and time at some period *before the onsite session*. This could mean 11:59 p.m. the day before the onsite, or simply an hour ahead of the onsite. Save enough time for teacher review of the quiz results before class.

The teacher can then share anonymous results onsite, and base activities or discussion on confusing or problematic questions.

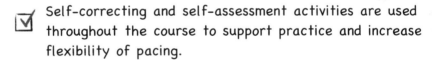

Self-correcting and self-assessment activities are used throughout the course to support practice and increase flexibility of pacing.

Self-assessment activities provide corrective feedback for incorrect answers and elaboration for correct answers.

7.5 Weaving Content-Driven Activities

Because a blended course consists of both onsite and online activities and events, teachers must deliberately connect these activities to bridge the spaces. With content-driven activities, teachers can weave activities by pointing out how practice activities directly connect to content, worked examples, and presentations. All activities should relate to specific learning outcomes by leading students to perform successfully on assessments.

Teachers should make these relationships clear by referencing back to learning that has happened in the past, and looking forward to learning or assessments that will happen in the future. Hyperlinking, which we will discuss in Chapter 9, will support this weaving.

 Online activities reference and connect with onsite activities, and vice versa.

7.6 Summary and Standards

Content-driven activities tend to benefit from online delivery, providing teachers the flexibility to move a significant amount of traditionally onsite activities online (Table 7.3). Lectures, presentations, and worked examples can be digitized and shared online, providing a resource that both students and teachers can reuse. Special care should be taken to ensure that presentations of all kinds are as engaging and effective as possible, whether done online or onsite. "Hands-on" activities may be one activity that teachers choose to reserve for onsite sessions, depending on the learning outcomes and the content.

All presentation of new information should be followed by activities that give students a chance to test their knowledge and apply learning. One example of this is to add self-assessments leveraging LMS quizzing tools to provide computer-automated scoring and repeated attempts.

Content-driven activities focus on presentation of new information, demonstration of skills, and opportunities to reinforce or practice. In the next chapter, we focus on blending community-driven activities, which encourage individual reflection, group discussion, and collaboration.

Table 7.3 Summary of onsite versus online advantages of major content-driven activities

Type of Activity	Onsite Advantages	Online Advantages
Lectures, presentations, and worked examples	Sensory richness Spontaneity Opportunities for elaboration	Flexibility of time and space Reusability User control of pacing
"Hands-on" guided practice	Simultaneous monitoring of whole class High level of "humanness" Allows for shared physical objects	No limits with simulations and virtual environments Supports individualized practice User control of pacing
Self-assessment quizzes	Easier to control against cheating	Individualized question selection Automated scoring Automatic feedback Multiple attempts

☐ Resources and activities support learning outcomes.

☐ Activities are frequent and varied.

☐ Activities encourage interactions that involve course content and personal communication.

☐ Audio and video material appearing within a lesson should be brief.

☐ Blocks of information are broken up into incremental chunks to support memory.

☐ New information, including teacher feedback, is followed by opportunities for students to apply the information.

☐ Stories, anecdotes, emotion, or human conflict are used to engage learners and show real-world relevance when appropriate.

☐ Content is designed to be simple and clear so as to avoid information overload (e.g. avoid narrating while written text is visible, using distracting images for decoration, presenting too much information at once, etc.).

☐ Presentations are designed to engage and support learner attention.

☐ Pedagogical steps build progressively, one upon the other, as is appropriate to the subject matter.

☐ Non-essential materials that may present extraneous cognitive load are avoided.

☐ Resource material is accessible to all students in commonly used formats.

☐ Materials are authentic or relate to real-life applications.

☐ Presentations include examples, models, case studies, illustrations, etc. for clarification.

☐ Self-correcting and self-assessment activities are used throughout the course to support practice and increase flexibility of pacing.

☐ Self-assessment activities provide corrective feedback for incorrect answers and elaboration for correct answers.

☐ Online activities reference and connect with onsite activities, and vice versa.

References and Further Reading

Anderson, T. (Ed.). (2008). *The theory and practice of online learning* (2nd ed.). Edmonton, Canada: Athabasca University Press.

Clark, R. C., Nguyen, F., & Sweller, J. (2006). *Efficiency in learning: Evidence-based guidelines to manage cognitive load.* San Francisco, CA: Pfeiffer.

deWinstanley, P. A., & Bjork, R. A. (2002). Successful lecturing: Presenting information in ways that engage effective processing. *New Directions for Teaching and Learning*, 89, 19–31. doi:10.1002/tl.44.

Ebert-May, D., Brewer, C., & Allred, S. (1997). Innovation in large lectures: Teaching for active learning. *BioScience*, 47(9), 601–607.

Holmberg, B. (1999). The conversational approach to distance education. *Open Learning*, 14(3), 58–60.

Karpicke, J. D., & Blunt, J. R. (2011). Retrieval practice produces more learning than elaborative studying with concept mapping. *Science (New York, N.Y.)*, 331(6018), 772–725. doi:10.1126/science.1199327.

Kirschner, P. A., Sweller, J., & Clark, R. E. (2006). Why minimal guidance during instruction does not work: An analysis of the failure of constructivist, discovery, problem-based, experiential, and inquiry-based teaching. *Educational Psychologist*, 41(2), 75–86.

Medina, J. (2009). *Brain rules: 12 principles for surviving and thriving at work, home, and school.* Seattle, WA: Pear Press.

Muller, D. A. (2008). *Designing effective multimedia for physics education* (doctoral dissertation). University of Sydney, Australia.

Chapter 8

Blending Community-Driven Learning Activities

Communities of practice are groups of people who share a concern or a passion for something they do and learn how to do it better as they interact regularly.

Etienne Wenger (2007)

We become ourselves through others.

Vygotsky (1966)

8.1 Why Community-Driven Activities Matter

Community-driven activities encourage learners to explore, share, analyze, and refine their thinking and practice through social interaction. They emphasize the social aspect of being human, and capitalize on learning effects that may capitalize on affective responses. Community-driven activities tend to target higher-level cognitive skills often enshrouded as "critical thinking" (e.g. application, analysis, evaluation, and creation).

Like content-driven learning activities, community-driven activities also tend to gain significant advantages when done online. However, because they involve person-to-person interaction, some of the innate attributes of face-to-face interactions may provide additional benefits that may lead teachers to choose to lead some of these activities in-class.

 To Do

Continue to develop plans for your prototype lesson using the course design map. By the end of this chapter, you should have enough ideas and notes in your course design map to begin building one blended lesson in your online environment.

Table 8.1 The general strengths and weaknesses of onsite and online environments with respect to interaction

	Onsite	Online
Strengths	**Human connection:** It is easier to bond and develop a social presence in a face-to-face environment. It makes it easier to develop trust. **Spontaneity:** Allow the generation of rapid chains of associated ideas and serendipitous discoveries.	**Flexibility:** Students can contribute to the discussion at the time and place that is most convenient for them. **Participation:** All students can participate because time and place constraints are removed. **Depth of reflection:** Learners have time to more carefully consider and provide evidence for their claims and provide deeper, more thoughtful reflections.
Weaknesses	**Participation:** Everyone cannot always participate, especially if the class is large and/or there are dominating personalities. **Flexibility:** Time is limited, which means that you may not be able to reach the discussion depth that you would like	**Spontaneity:** The generation of rapid chains of ideas and serendipitous discoveries is not encouraged. **Procrastination:** There may be a tendency towards procrastination when students have increased flexibility and autonomy. **Human connection:** The medium is considered to be impersonal. This may cause a lower satisfaction level with the communication.

Some of these onsite benefits have to do with the human connection—the sense of empathy, social energy, or shared experience—which can be used to develop affective outcomes and engage the heart (Table 8.1).

As we've done in previous chapters, we'll consider the relative strengths and weaknesses of online versus onsite modes for each of the community-driven learning activities.

8.2 Blogs and Learning Journals

I write to know what I think.

Joan Didion

Learning journals are chronologically organized spaces where the learner can:

- Summarize learning.
- Situate new knowledge in context of existing understanding.
- Reflect upon past efforts and future goals for learning.

Blogs, from "Web logs," are personalized, open, online authoring spaces geared toward community discussion (through commenting) and engagement (through subscription and response posts).

Learning journals are typically content-driven. However, they cross the boundary to community-driven activities when done through blogs.

The Web makes online journaling a natural fit. Traditionally, learning journals have been composed with text, making them another vehicle to practice writing and communication skills. Easy access to multimedia authoring tools and publishing on the Web can change and enhance the learning journal.

Blogs are one way the traditional learning journal can be transformed. Blogs are bigger than learning journals, encompassing more activities, and focusing on sharing. Table 8.2 shows some distinctions between blogs and journals in how they are typically used.

Table 8.2 Comparison of traditional learning journals and blogs

	Journal	Blog
Audience	Teacher, learner	Teacher, learner, peers, others
Content	Journal entries (personal reflections, summaries)	Journal entries, reviews, showcase works, opinion pieces, etc.
Access	Closed (private)	Open (public)
Space	Teacher-owned, e.g. Learning Management System (LMS)	Student-owned, e.g. blog platform
Lifespan	Terminal (semester)	Indefinite

Blogging

What Happens?

Students post articles, reviews, works, or journal entries to their blog, where teachers, classmates, and others read and comment on these posts.

Why?

Blogs serve the learning outcomes associated with learning journals and beyond, depending on their usage. Blogs add some key advantages in that they are truly student-owned, can reach a larger audience, and may exert positive pressure on learners to compose quality content in their posts.

The commenting feature of blogs allows others to give public feedback, guidance, praise, etc. The public nature of blogs and blog commenting encourages *network effects* that build professional and personal connections with others.

Blogs are designed to have an indefinite lifespan, and are thus well suited to serve as a seamless record of learning both within an academic program and across the curriculum.

Where?

On a student's own blog, through popular blogging platforms such as WordPress.com, Blogger.com, Posterous.com, or through their own personal website.

Who?

Typically individual students, but groups or the entire class can collectively blog.

How?

Students each create a blog on a blogging platform. The teacher collects the URLs of the students' blogs, and shares these with the class either as a simple list or as a Web feed. The teacher also provides some direction to students on frequency and content of blog posts to fulfill learning outcomes.

Learners compose and publish posts to their own blog. Blog posts can be automatically "delivered" to teachers and other learners via Web feeds in a news reader. Open discussion of the post happens in the comments section.

A news reader, or feed reader, collects website feeds from any number of different blogs or news sources, and delivers them in an easy-to-read online format through a Web browser or mobile device.

Teachers can assess and score posts privately, through the assignment or grades feature of an LMS.

The key advantage of journaling is privacy, but blogs, too, can provide limited access to all or certain posts through the use of passwords.

Student Privacy and Online Publishing

Many countries have law that protects students' rights to privacy in the sphere of education. For example, under FERPA in the US, teachers cannot publish class enrollments, student work, or grades without explicit permission of the students. Thus, teachers wishing to use blogs in their classroom should both advise students of their FERPA rights, and give them the option to post privately (e.g. password-protected) or with an alias. Remember: students *can* choose to publish personally identifiable information themselves, but it is the teacher's obligation to give students options if they wish not to.

 Activities allow students to retain their privacy on their own terms.

Activity: Reading Reviews

The information students read can be reinforced and explored when summarized and analyzed through writing. Directing students to write about the things they are reading—from chapters in their textbook to articles related to their research or interests—is a good way to leverage blogs (Figure 8.1). In this case, the blog provides both a record of the work for the student to reference later, and a space for discussion of the students' reaction and analysis.

Teachers should prompt students to review their reading regularly on their blog. Reviews can be casual in order to encourage the activity as a habit rather than an assignment.

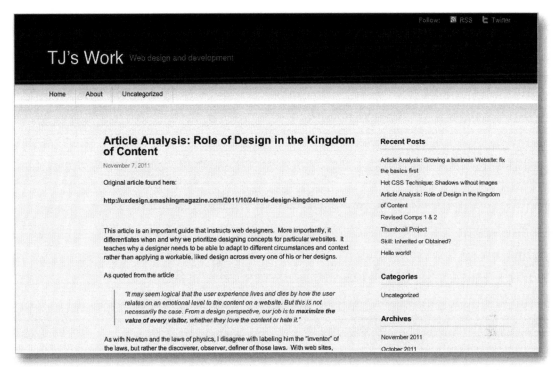

Figure 8.1 A student's article analysis, posted to her blog

Community discussion can be optional, but should be emphasized when students are working through difficult materials together, or are exploring different topics that might be of interest to their peers.

Activity: Collaborative Class Blog

There are numerous examples of successful class blogging projects, where the teacher sets up and maintains the blog as a publication of learning and discovery for a course topic (Figure 8.2). In a class blog, the teacher may act as an editor, or students themselves may be assigned editorial roles.

Students are assigned topics to post on, either individually or in small groups, throughout the semester. Students are directed to comment on the class posts throughout the semester, making the comment space of each blog post a mini-discussion forum.

Students may also be encouraged to share the blog with others outside the class, offering an insight into the workings of the class, as well as the potential for class members to connect with others learning or working in the field.

When a class blog persists beyond a single semester, it creates a fascinating record of the life cycle of the course, and provides additional context and examples for current students.

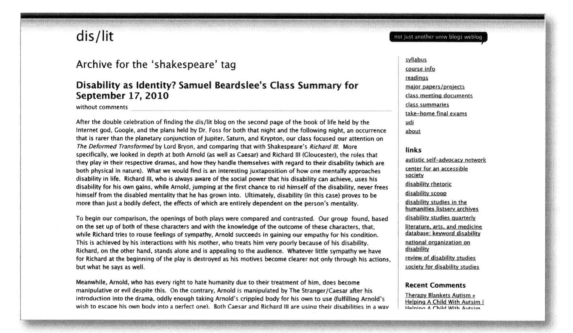

Figure 8.2 A collaborative class blog at University of Mary Washington: Chris Foss's Disability and Literature (dislit2012.umwblogs.org)

Tip

While traditional blogging platforms such as WordPress.com and Blogger.com support both text and multimedia, some social media sites are specially built for uploading, publishing, and sharing multimedia. Consider Flickr.com for photos or illustrations, and YouTube.com or Vimeo.com for video.

☑ Reflection and reflective activities come up throughout the course.

☑ When blogs are used, they are established as learner-owned spaces for sharing and discussion.

Students are encouraged to share resources as is appropriate.

8.3 Synchronous Peer Instruction

Onsite time is precious in a blended course. Peer instruction, as developed and refined by Eric Mazur of Harvard University, focuses in-class time on specific learning trouble spots while building community and giving all students a chance to prove or change their understanding. This encourages students to take responsibility for their own learning by sufficiently preparing and being able to explain their learning. It also provides an opportunity for students to support — and even take responsibility for — the learning of others.

For the sake of efficiency, peer instruction needs spontaneous, synchronous interaction, making it less viable online.

Instant Polling with Clickers, Phones, or Hand-Signals

Mazur's peer instruction method uses *student response systems*, or "clickers" — small, remote control-type devices that instantly relay individual student responses to questions to the teacher's computer. With a multiple-choice question on screen, students press their answer choice on their clicker, and the results are then shown via a teacher display or projector.

Clickers are not necessarily required for this activity, however. Some student response systems now use software that's installed on a phone or other mobile device. The LMS may provide a mobile interface that allows online quizzes and polls to serve the same purpose. A low-tech solution is to have each student make a hand signal near their chest to show their answer choice (e.g. three fingers for answer choice number three).

Peer Instruction

What Happens?

Based on student feedback on the most challenging topics for the week, the teacher presents a multiple-choice question to the class (Figure 8.3). Using either mobile devices, student response systems (aka "clickers"), or even just hand signals, students individually "vote" for an answer choice.

The teacher does not reveal the correct answer, but if a significant number of students choose the wrong answer, students partner with a classmate sitting next to them, and debate the possible choices. Once they have agreed upon an answer, students vote again and the cycle continues.

The teacher may wrap up a question with direct instruction or a worked example, or may simply move on to the next question.

Why?

By basing the questions on topics the students say were challenging or difficult, the teacher can spend precious onsite time focusing just on the trouble spots. When students respond to the question onsite, the teacher has immediate confirmation that the topic is troublesome; otherwise, she moves on. By requiring students to debate the answer choices with a peer, they must both "rehearse" the information as they understand it, and examine and correct each other's understanding. Mastery is ensured by cycling through the question, response, and debate format until understanding surpasses the threshold.

Where?

In the classroom.

How?

- Ahead of the onsite session, students are instructed to study a topic, perhaps a reading or video lectures.
- Students respond to a pre-class quiz, discussion topic, or poll that identifies any challenging areas, troublesome topics, or difficult concepts.
- Based on the student responses, the teacher creates a multiple-choice question for each difficult concept. These may be prepared as presentation slides with clicker software, as poll-type questions in an LMS, or simply as questions on the whiteboard.

Peer Instruction: Magnetic Striping

The magnetic striping of the seafloor is considered evidence of seafloor spreading and...

1. ...periodic reversals in the polarity of the Earth's magnetic field.

2. ...spreading centers in the trenches.

3. ...subduction down the rift valleys.

4. ...changes in the Earth's axis of rotation.

Figure 8.3 A multiple-choice question is shared with the class when used for peer instruction

- In-class, the teacher may review the concept, or go straight to the question.
- After a minute to think the question through, students must each signal their response.
- The teacher shows the response on screen.
- If 85 percent or more of the class chose the correct answer, the teacher moves on. If less, students are asked to turn to the person next to them and talk through the question until they agree on an answer. If less than 30 percent of the class chooses the correct answer, then that is a signal to provide direct instruction, skipping the peer discussion phase.
- After a few minutes, students are directed to signal their agreed-upon response, and the process repeats until the mastery threshold is met.

Tip

Online peer instruction activities could be accomplished using video conferencing on the Web, with live polling. Some LMSs may have videoconferencing either built-in or integrated.

☑ Learners take responsibility for their learning and, at times, the learning of others.

8.4 Class Discussions

> Learning does not belong to individual persons, but to the
> various conversations of which they are a part.
>
> McDermott (1999)

Class discussions provide opportunities for teachers to direct student exploration of a topic, and for students to test ideas, ask questions, and debate points. Class discussions foster the development of *community*, which is fundamental to student learning in the higher levels of the cognitive domain (Garrison & Archer 2000).

Tip
Create (or encourage students to create) an open forum where students can organize study sessions, meet outside of formal class activities, or simply build a sense of community through social interaction.

Discussions can be formal (e.g. topic-based, teacher-directed, and participation-required), or informal (e.g. the topic varies depending on the needs of the students, the learning community collaborates on responses, and participation is not required).

Class discussions have distinct advantages both onsite and online. Depending on what you need learners to accomplish, you may choose the strengths of one or the other, or mix the two through a bridging activity.

In a blended course, online discussion forums can be used in many of the same ways as in an online course, so we will focus on ways of using discussion forums in a blended environment that enhance and transform.

Online Discussions

What Happens?

Online class discussions in a blended course let students engage asynchronously, but within a time frame—typically, the space between one class meeting and another. These discussions are usually led or started by one class member—typically, the teacher, but not always.

A blended course's online discussions may be another layer of the class experience, or may be interwoven with onsite discussions (see "Activity: Bridging Discussions" on p. 156 as an example).

Why?

Much has been written elsewhere about various strategies for employing online discussion forums in online classes. The key advantages of online discussion forums include:

- **Inclusiveness.** When you remove constraints of the face-to-face classroom, you will find all students can participate, and many students who may have been reluctant to speak up can be active members of the conversation.
- **Reflection.** Onsite discussions have to be rapid-fire. There is not much time for reflection. When students take time to think through and even research their response, their contributions are more reflective and substantial.
- **Positive social pressure.** The online discussion forum creates a space where students' contributions are on record. This encourages students to carefully craft their posts and engage in critical thinking about others.
- **Delineation.** An online discussion forum allows students to start from a single topic and still diverge to focus on angles or facets of the topic that most interest them. **As a moderator, it is your job to help them tie these divergences back to the main idea.**
- **Participation tracking.** If your students can earn points toward their grade by participating in discussions, the online environment makes it easier to track, evaluate, and link discussion performance to an online grade book.

Where?

Online discussions usually happen in a discussions tool, often within an LMS. This space usually consists of a topic with nested "threads" to show the direction of student responses.

Online discussions can also happen in the comments area of blog posts, or in the discussion section of a wiki.

Who?

The entire class, or the class divided into groups.

How?

The teacher sets up the topic by creating a forum in the discussions tool of the LMS. This may be a single question to the class or a more general topic of conversation. Clear directions to the students for engaging in the discussion will help set expectations.

Students respond to both the original discussion prompt as well as to each other's responses. Responses can be text, audio, or video, depending on the tools readily available to you.

At least initially, teachers can expect to be heavily involved in the discussions, both guiding students toward course goals, and modeling good responses and follow-up questions.

Activity: Topic Discussions

Summarizing and expressing new knowledge is a great way to develop true understanding and reinforce the kinds of mental schemata that are critical for effective learning. This is one reason why online discussions are so valuable: they provide an opportunity for *every* class member to reflect upon, explain, question, and explore what they've learned.

Tip

Experts from outside the class can be invited to join a specific class discussion to offer their experience and insight. If done onsite, you should consider recording the event for online sharing later. If done online, the guest can take advantage of the flexibility provided by discussion forums to post when most convenient.

Creating a regular, online topic-based discussion connects course content and specific topics with social interaction through personal communication. Teachers designate the topic and provide directions that set expectations (Figure 8.4). Students engage throughout the time frame set for discussion—setting a time frame is important in online courses, as it ensures the class moves forward together. But a time frame is critical in a blended course, where the rhythm of the class is based on regular, face-to-face sessions.

The teacher may assess online discussion participation, resulting in a score. In such cases, a rubric is valuable both for setting expectations and providing feedback (see Chapter 6).

Tip

In large classes, divide students into groups that can each have their own online discussion space. This limits the redundancy of replies, prevents students from being overwhelmed by the volume of responses, and allows for more personal engagement.

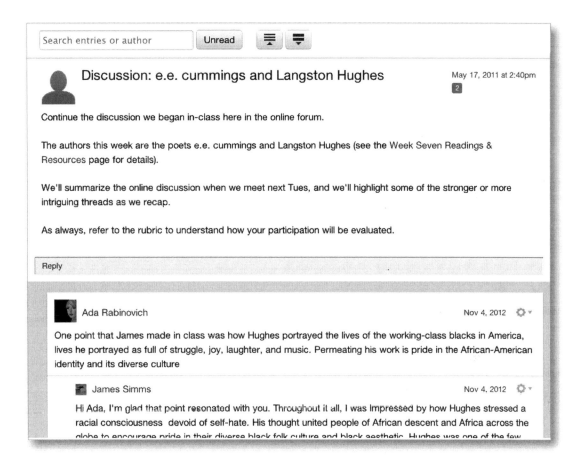

Figure 8.4 Students participating in an online topic-based discussion

Variation: Pre-Class Q&A

An online Q&A forum can be set up for each week or lesson as an open space for students to express what they are struggling with and what confuses them (Figure 8.5). This can provide the teacher with important feedback that can guide instruction or help plan activities for the onsite sessions.

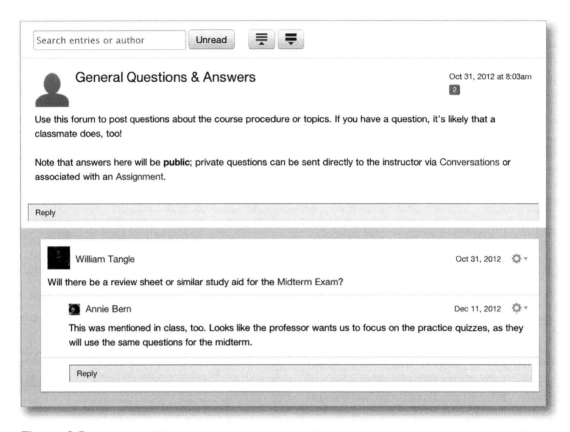

Figure 8.5 A general Q&A forum lets you leverage the community, and share answers with the class

A pre-class Q&A forum can be optional or required: students may be asked to post when they encounter difficult topics or confounding questions, or students may be required to post at the end of a lesson, sharing what they want to learn more about.

 An online space (e.g. discussion board, social network) is in place for students to meet outside the class.

Onsite Discussions

Onsite discussions have the advantage of speed: a discussion can be started in-class simply by the teacher announcing it — no need to log in to an LMS and create a new topic that students must then login to visit. Onsite discussions are also credited with greater spontaneity, which may lead to useful tangents and happy accidents of discovery.

Onsite discussions also have the advantage of sensory richness of a physical environment. The face-to-face nature fosters the humanness and empathy that often accompanies seeing and hearing each other. While all of these traits *can* be built into online discussions, careful planning or encouragement may be required.

Activity: Bridging Discussions

For courses that rely heavily on deep, fully engaged class discussions, a bridging format is ideal in a blended course. From the beginning of the semester, students learn to connect onsite discussions to online discussions, and vice versa.

Following the topics of the course schedule, each onsite meeting includes a guided discussion of a topic. This allows for all of the advantages of face to face. At the end of the allotted time, the teacher prompts students to continue or expand the discussion in the online forum.

The online discussion is much like the topic discussion described above, and is designed to move the onsite discussion to higher cognitive levels. Discussion continues in the online forum in the space between class sessions (Figure 8.6). This provides all the strengths of the online format.

Continue the discussion we began in-class here in the online forum focusing on this week's authors (see this week's *Readings & Resources* page for details).

Use this space to elaborate on points that we didn't spend a lot of time on in class. Return to the texts and consult other works to add additional perspectives.

When we meet in-class next Tuesday we'll wrap up and highlight the more intriguing threads from the online discussion.

As always, refer to the rubric to understand how your participation will be evaluated.

Figure 8.6 Instructions for an online "bridging" discussion that links in-class dialogue with online, and vice versa.

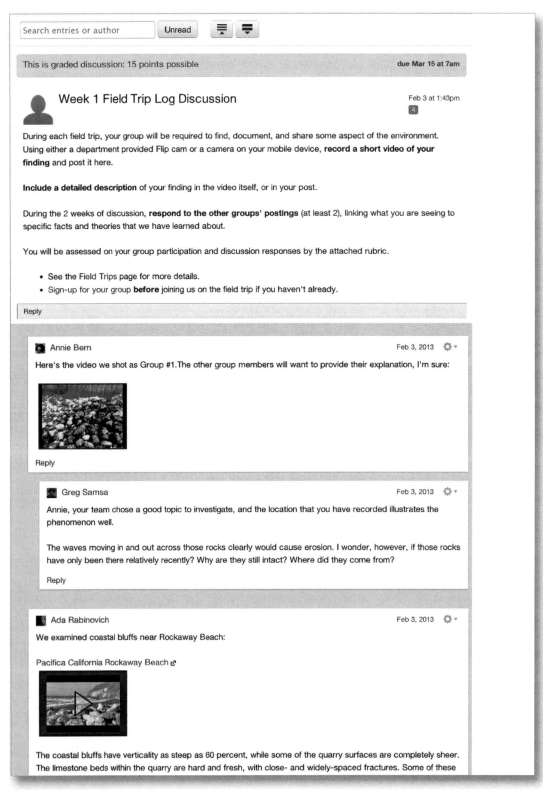

Figure 8.7 This example bridges onsite field trips to online reflection and discussion

When the class next meets, the teacher may summarize the online discussion or highlight certain posts or threads in order to provide feedback and additional information. From there, a new discussion topic may be introduced, or the current topic may continue.

☑ **Activities encourage active interactions that involve course content and personal communication.**

☑ **Discussions are designed to capitalize on the asynchronous nature of online and the synchronous nature of onsite.**

Assessing Discussions

While online discussions are primarily used as learning activities, they may also be used as evidence of learning for assessment purposes. Some teachers may simply want to give students credit for participating in discussions as a score in the grade book. An LMS might provide discussion forums that can automatically calculate scores based on quantity of posts (e.g. students might be required to post three times per week). But this doesn't address quality and the more subjective judgments of interaction and engagement. For these purposes, you can use a rubric to both set student expectations for participation and facilitate scoring of student performance (Figure 6.3).

Discussion forums may even be where peer reviews take place (Figure 8.8). Instead of one-to-one peer reviews, open peer reviews in a discussion forum allow everyone in the class to provide and benefit from feedback on an individual work. Community-centered peer reviews may create positive social pressure that softens criticism and encourages constructive feedback.

☑ **Learners are encouraged to interact with others (classmates, course guests, etc.) to benefit from their expertise.**

☑ **Criteria/rubrics clearly inform learners as to how they will be assessed on specific assignments.**

This is graded discussion: 20 points possible   due -

Web Site Map & Task Flow
Jared Stein
                                                                                  Mar 24 at 6:41pm

In our last face-to-face session we workshopped your client's web site definition, objective, and strategy. Now it's time to begin developing the user experience by mapping out the actual web site based on user task flows.

You're responsible for drafting a web site map as described in this week's lesson. Make it professional easy to understand, so your client will quickly get on board. Your site map should be...

1. **User-focused.** Map the key user paths to their destination(s). This gives you an idea of the user experience.
2. **Thorough.** Your client should not be able to see any missing elements.
3. **Logical.** Relationships between pages and objects should be obvious, and paths should be short. To quote Steve Krug, "Don't make me think!"
4. **Meaningful.** Use shapes, colors, connectors (lines), fonts, and text descriptively and consistently.

When we meet face-to-face next week we'll used these web site maps to create user scenarios that will illustrate the task flows.

Create your site map in any media or program that allows for diagramming, such as Microsoft Excel, bubbl.us ⤢ , etc.

To submit your assignment you must **Reply** here and...

- Attach your document (XLS/XLSX, JPG, PNG, or PDF only), *OR*
- Post the assignment to your blog or web site and share the hyperlink

Examples

Here are two examples from previous semesters. One is an "A" the other a "B":

- Project 02 - Y ⤢
- Project 02 - Z ⤢

Don't forget to remind us what your site is about by including the **one sentence** objective and strategy from last week's project.

Ideas for Discussion

As projects begin to be posted, read and respond to at least 2 of your classmates' projects.

Here are some ideas:

- How would you react as a client?
- How would a user accomplish their task? Are their faster routes than those shown in the map?
- Count the number of clicks it would take for a user to get to prime content. Compare that to the number of clicks it takes to get to similar content on competitors' web sites.

Figure 8.8 This project is submitted via the discussion forum in order to encourage students to provide feedback to their classmates on their work

8.5   Weaving Community-Driven Activities

Weaving community-driven activities is often easier because you have more weavers: the students. Here are some tips on successful weaving:

- **Blogging.** Highlight outstanding blog posts onsite, or point out blog posts that deserve more commentary. Encourage students to post their personal notes from lectures or onsite activities to their blogs—however rough.

- **Class discussion.** Bridging discussions is an explicit example of how community-driven activities can be woven between onsite and online experiences. Onsite discussions should leverage online resources—especially if students have access to the Internet in class. Online discussions should encourage students to reference in-class activities or discoveries.
- **Peer instruction.** Assess student's mastery before class with online quizzes. Provide the discussion problems online *afterward* for review.

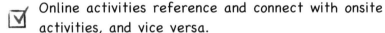 Online activities reference and connect with onsite activities, and vice versa.

8.6 Summary and Standards

Community-driven activities can be done online or onsite. Online discussions offer students flexibility with time and

Table 8.3 Summary of onsite versus online advantages of major community-driven activities

Type of Activity	Onsite Advantages	Online Advantages
Blogging		Encourages active thinking Builds a chronology of work Publishing is in online space on the open Web
Peer Instruction	Few technology barriers More efficient Benefits from synchronous presence	Leverages online polling Stores results digitally
Class or group discussions	High level of "humanness" Spontaneous synergy	Flexibility of time and space Encourages reflection and research Easier to assess Grade book integration

increase opportunities to participate. Onsite discussions can be started on the fly, and provide a sense of humanness and empathy that is harder to capture online. Peer instruction, as described by Eric Mazur, is best suited for onsite because it relies on synchronous interaction between students. However, we note that synchronous interaction is possible via videoconferencing on the Web. Blogging is the one community-driven activity described here that seems to have little place in the face-to-face environment, since it straddles the boundaries between content-driven and community-driven activities.

☐ Activities allow students to retain their privacy on their own terms.

☐ Reflection and reflective activities come up throughout the course.

☐ When blogs are used, they are established as learner-owned spaces for sharing and discussion.

☐ Students are encouraged to share resources as is appropriate.

☐ Learners take responsibility for their learning and, at times, the learning of others.

☐ An online space (e.g. discussion board, social network) is in place for students to meet outside the class.

☐ Activities encourage active interactions that involve course content and personal communication.

☐ Discussions are designed to capitalize on the asynchronous nature of online and the synchronous nature of onsite.

☐ Learners are encouraged to interact with others (classmates, course guests, etc.) to benefit from their expertise.

☐ Criteria/rubrics clearly inform learners as to how they will be assessed on specific assignments.

☐ Online activities reference and connect with onsite activities, and vice versa.

References and Further Reading

Diaz, V., & Initiative, E. L. (2010). Privacy considerations in cloud-based teaching and learning environments. ELI Paper 3. Educause. Retrieved from http://net.educause.edu/ir/library/pdf/ELI3024.pdf.

Ebert-May, D., Brewer, C., & Allred, S. (1997). Innovation in large lectures: Teaching for active learning. *BioScience*, 47(9), 601–607.

Foss, Chris. (2012). ENGL 375A2: Disability in literature. Retrieved from http://dislit2012.umwblogs.org.

Garrison, D. R., & Archer. W. (2000). *A transactional perspective on teaching-learning transaction: A framework for adult and higher education*. Oxford: Pergamon.

Garrison, D. R., & Cleveland-Innes, M. (2005). Cognitive presence in online learning: Interaction is not enough. *American Journal of Distance Education*, 19(3), 133–148.

Hall, H., & Davison, B. (2007). Social software as support in hybrid learning environments: The value of the blog as a tool for reflective learning and peer support. *Library and Information Science Research*, 29, 163–187.

Johnson, E. J., & Card, K. (2008). The effects of instructor and student immediacy behaviors in writing improvement and course satisfaction in a web-based undergraduate course. *MountainRise, The International Journal of the Scholarship of Teaching and Learning*, 4(2), 1–21.

Kessler, P. D., & Lund, C. H. (2004). Reflective journaling: Developing an online journal for distance education. *Nurse Educator*, 29(1), 20–24.

McDermott, R. P. (1999). On becoming labelled: The story of Adam. In P. Murphy (Ed.), *Learners, learning, and assessment* (pp. 1–21). London: Paul Chapman Publishing, Ltd.

Sands, P. (2002). Inside outside, upside downside: Strategies for connecting online and face-to-face instruction in hybrid courses. *Teaching with Technology Today*, 8(6). Retrieved from www.uwsa.edu/ttt/articles/sands2.htm.

Vygotsky, L. S. (1966). Development of higher mental functions. In A. N. Leontyev, A. R. Luria, & A. Smirnov (Eds.), *Psychological Research in the USSR*. Moscow: Progress Publishers.

Wenger, E. (c 2007). Communities of practice: A brief introduction. In *Communities of practice*. Retrieved from www.ewenger.com/theory.

Chapter 9 | Weaving it All Together

> Future learning systems may not be differentiated as much based on *whether* they blend but rather by *how* they blend.
>
> Barbara Ross and Karen Gage, *Global Perspectives on Blended Learning*

A blended course experience consists of activities and assessments that span the onsite and online environments. Because much of the learning time happens online, the online environment should consist of an intuitive navigation that immediately engages students in relevant, contextualized activities. The online environment also provides a great way of providing clear, explicit information for students that sets expectations and serves as a reference for the duration of the course.

 To Do

At this point, you should have at least one lesson planned out (goals, outcomes, assessments, activities) using the course design map template. This chapter will help you use your plan to build out a lesson prototype within your Learning Management System (LMS) or course website.

9.1 | A Lesson Prototype

The backward design process we have described in this guide (i.e. starting with learning outcomes before designing assessments that lead to learning activities) can be followed to produce a prototype lesson within your LMS or course website. A single lesson prototype can then serve as the model for all other lessons in the course.

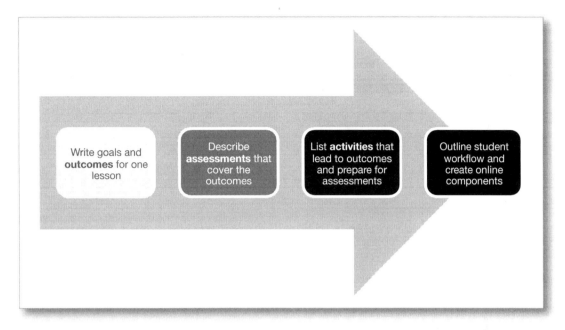

Figure 9.1 The backward design process leads you to create a prototype lesson, the major unit of a course

While we can't provide a tutorial on building within an LMS (since all LMSs are different), we will guide you through the activities and principles that you will need to construct a single prototype lesson for use in your blended course.

 See the website for a list of LMSs, including some that are free for teachers.

Modules versus Folders

Most LMSs provide "module" or "folder" metaphors for organizing materials and activities. **Modules are better for lessons**, as they provide a structure that can sequence content, activities, and assessments. Modules create a linear path that is easy for students to follow (Figure 9.1).

Folders are better for non-sequential content, e.g. a set of examples or collected resources (Figure 9.2). Students will need clear directions to use specific items in folders so they know when to access them, and for what purpose.

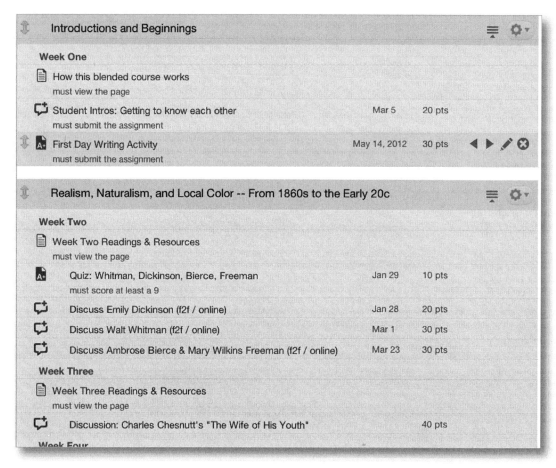

Figure 9.2 "Modules" help you sequence resources and activities to guide students through the course

Engaging and Orienting Students with a Lesson Introduction

Each lesson should begin with an introduction that explains the structure and flow. The introductory lesson page should:

- Get students' attention with a story or case study that gives real-world meaning to desired learning outcomes.
- Prime students' thinking by proposing a question or challenge.
- Outline required tasks for the lesson using numbers to indicate sequential order.
- Indicate which lesson tasks will be done onsite versus online.
- Link to the next activity in the lesson.
- Link back to the course home page.

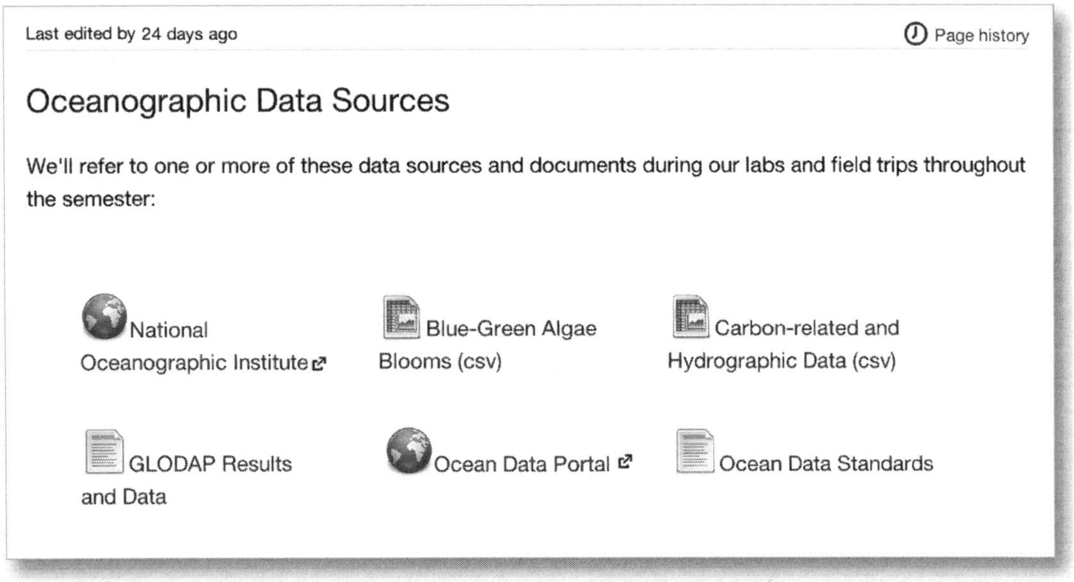

Figure 9.3 A "folder" or "page" links to organized—but non-sequential—materials

Tip

Embedding video or other multimedia on the introductory lesson page is a great way to engage students' attention, elicit their existing knowledge of a subject, and help them understand how the lesson connects to the real world.

Tip

Marking activities with a simple convention such as "f2f" or "web" throughout your lessons can help students know where to expect the engagement to take place.

Lesson introductions are most effective when they are concise and easily understood. Throughout your course website, but especially when providing instructions, the writing style should be clear, concise, and to the point. Any time tasks or steps in a process are provided, numbers should be used to indicate sequence or priority.

- ☑ Lessons are introduced with stories, case studies, questions, or challenges to engage students' attention and make outcomes meaningful.
- ☑ Introductions and summaries are provided at the beginning and end of units.
- ☑ Instructions and requirements are stated simply, clearly, and logically.

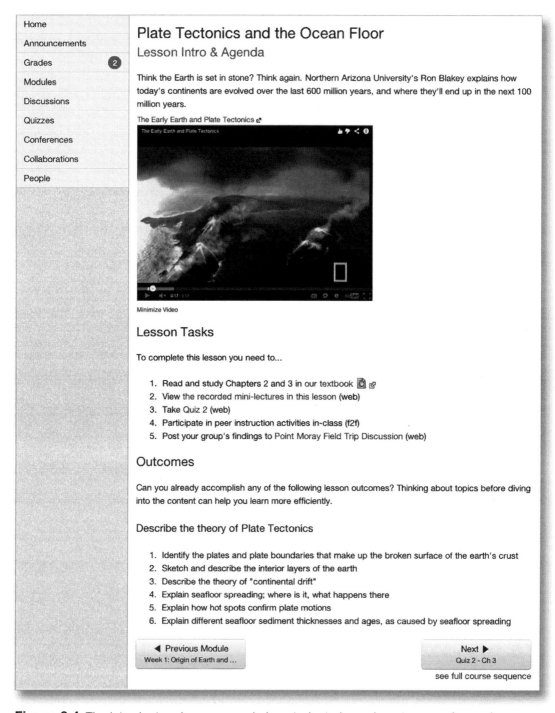

Figure 9.4 The introductory lesson page helps students know how to move forward

☑ The writing style is clear, concise, and direct.

☑ Numbers are used to identify sequential steps in a task or process.

Weaving with Hyperlinks

Hyperlinks are what make the Web. They add dimension to information by connecting web pages to other pages or websites that relate, connect, or even contrast.

Note

Too many hyperlinks can be distracting, and may increase unnecessary cognitive overload. Hyperlinks that are non-essential to the lesson can lead students away from the task at hand.

In a blended course, hyperlinks make it easy for students to navigate from one part of the course to another, or simply to see how one activity relates to past or future activities. We recommend using *relevant* hyperlinks that support navigation throughout your blended course website.

Some LMSs make it easy for you to link to other parts of the course website by providing an index of course topics and activities that you can click to select. Some web page text editors allow you to copy and paste or drag and drop links or web pages directly into the content. Few require that you know HTML.

Research note: Gerbic (2009) stresses that there should be a "strong integration between [blended course] components: weekly topics or course content pointing to discussion, teacher feedback about progress or performance, practice in the f2f meeting."

Experiment with the text editor that your LMS or website provides so you are confident in creating hyperlinks throughout your course.

☑ Materials consistently indicate when activities or assessments take place onsite versus online.

☑ Direct links are provided to course materials and resources.

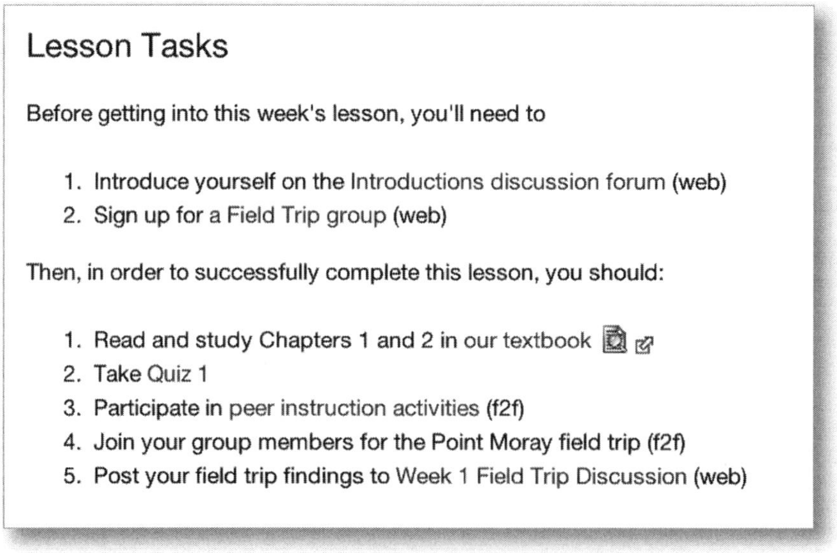

Lesson Tasks

Before getting into this week's lesson, you'll need to

1. Introduce yourself on the Introductions discussion forum (web)
2. Sign up for a Field Trip group (web)

Then, in order to successfully complete this lesson, you should:

1. Read and study Chapters 1 and 2 in our textbook
2. Take Quiz 1
3. Participate in peer instruction activities (f2f)
4. Join your group members for the Point Moray field trip (f2f)
5. Post your field trip findings to Week 1 Field Trip Discussion (web)

Figure 9.5 Hyperlinks ease navigation and provide context

Organizing Lesson Activities Online

The lesson introduction page in a blended course clearly outlines the activities students must complete, whether online or onsite. The rest of the lesson can be easily constructed online based on this outline.

First, you'll need to upload or create the individual components of the lesson:

- **Materials** (such as required readings or supplements for onsite activities) are uploaded to the course's file repository.
- **Pages** are constructed to organize and contextualize materials, resources, and activities.
- **Learning activities** (such as discussion forums, assignments, self-assessments, practice exercises, etc.) are created with clear instructions.
- **Assessments** are built using online tools such as assignments with drop boxes, quizzes, etc.

Then, organize these lesson components by *sequence*. **Organizing by activity type is a common mistake**, as it does not encourage linear progression, and, in fact, can impede student progress through the lesson.

Content elements are presented in a logical sequence.

9.2 The Course Home Page as a Hub

Why does a student go to the course website? Invariably, it is to accomplish a task, such as to:

- View feedback or scores on assessments.
- Work on a learning activity.
- Complete an assessment.

A blended course's home page should direct students to whatever tasks are **most relevant to them at the time that they visit**. For example, the home page may include:

- A full course schedule or complete listing of lessons, with hyperlinks to activities and assessments (Figure 9.6).
- Information on just the current lesson (Figure 9.7).
- A checklist of regular, weekly tasks—including onsite meetings (Figure 9.8).
- A dynamic list of the latest activity in the course (e.g. new discussions or feedback).

Tip
Always provide ways for students to quickly access grades, the course calendar, messaging, and other critical tools throughout the course website. These tools let students understand their progress and stay on task. Most LMSs provide such links by default.

Remember, students typically have to navigate through the home page *every time they visit*, so avoid wasting the home page on one-time information (such as a welcome message) or basic course information (such as the course summary, goals, or prerequisites) that is better suited for the general class announcement or the syllabus.

 The course website is organized to guide and direct students toward course goals.

Figure 9.6 This course home page presents a schedule of weekly activities

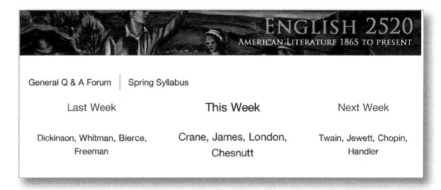

Figure 9.7 This course home page focuses student attention on the current week's lesson

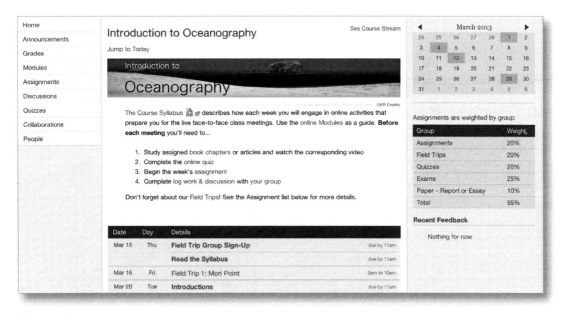

Figure 9.8 This course home page focuses on the regular and weekly tasks students will need to work on

9.3 Usability from Start to Finish

Because we want students to spend their time learning, not navigating the course website or struggling with online tools, it is important that course website materials are designed with usability in mind. This is challenging for any course designer, because we inherently understand our own design, and thus it tends to be simple to us. But it's not simple to everyone, especially not new students.

The key principle for usability is to **make everything as brief and simple as possible**. As usability expert Steve Krug (2006) puts it, "Don't make me think." This mantra is especially relevant for course websites, because we want students to spend their time thinking about the **subject**, not the interface.

You don't have to be a usability expert to design for usability. Two simple practices will help you design usable learning experiences:

- **Imagine your most challenged student working through the course website or lesson.** Will he know where to go without thinking? Will it always be clear what he should do next?

- **Have several people test the site out.** Try to use students, friends, or family members—not colleagues who are already experts in the subject area or are experienced teachers themselves. You can look over their shoulder, but don't help them drive—just ask them to find their way through a lesson or two and make a note of anything that holds them up or doesn't make sense.

Plan to make changes to your course site design, or even to the instructions for learning activities, based on the feedback you receive from others. You'll also want to include a question about usability in the instructional survey that we advise for blended courses in Chapter 10.

☑ The course website provides the shortest route for student navigation to relevant activities.

☑ The course website has been tested by non-experts to help identify any major usability problems.

9.4　Constructing the Blended Syllabus

The backward design model used in this guide leaves the construction of the blended course syllabus document until the end. Even if you begin with an existing syllabus, you'll find that the blended syllabus must be composed quite differently. But we've laid all the groundwork that we need for a great syllabus in Chapters 5–8, and much of the blended syllabus will now easily fall into place.

Just as there are many interpretations of what a syllabus should be, there are many ways to construct a syllabus. We think a course syllabus should reflect the course, and since blending a course constitutes a dramatic redesign of assessments and activities, it makes sense to write the syllabus as the course itself is written.

Some things will always be the foundation of a syllabus and can be added before a single blended lesson is designed:

- A course description (Chapter 5).
- Course goals (Chapter 5).
- Prerequisites or foundational knowledge (if any).
- Methods of contacting the teacher.
- Grading scheme.
- Course policies (e.g. consequences of plagiarism, cheating, etc.).
- Contact information to advisers or technical help at the school.

Technology Support and Technical Help

Be sure to describe how students can get technical help. This is critical in any course that relies heavily on technology. You may be able to refer students to a campus technology support line or distance education help desk. If that is not available, you may need to prepare yourself to field some technical questions. If you do, make it easier on yourself by: (1) providing a set of links to online tutorials or guides on using the LMS or website; and and (2) creating a "Students Helping Students" or "Q&A" discussion forum (see Chapter 8) where students are encouraged to post and respond to technical or course-related questions.

As a teacher, it's a good idea to have your own technology support plan, too. You don't want to find yourself stuck within the LMS with no idea of who to turn to.

Tip

Encourage students to *plan* for technology failure so it doesn't take them by surprise. Technology fails everyone at some point, but being prepared— turning work in early, knowing who to contact, having a "plan B"—will keep a failure from turning into a disaster.

Other elements of a syllabus can be added later, as you design and iterate lessons. For example:

- **a schedule** of topics, week by week;
- **an overview or walkthrough** of a typical week or lesson;
- **general descriptions** of regular activities and assessments;
- **your expectations** of student participation.

Each of these elements deserve special attention in a blended course, as students will need a clear understanding of what will take place onsite and what will happen online.

 A syllabus including contact information, an outline, requirements, and guidelines is accessible from the start of the course throughout.

 Syllabus orients students to class workflow by providing a descriptive overview or walkthrough of a typical lesson.

 Contact information to advisers and technical help is provided in the syllabus.

Course Schedule

Some LMSs will automatically generate a course schedule based on the due date-based assignments and events that you create in the course (Figure 9.8). In these cases, don't reinvent the wheel and produce a second schedule.

Otherwise, prepare a schedule in a simple-to-scan format, either by topic or by week. A course schedule in a blended course should include:

- The topic to be covered.
- Date/time of any onsite meeting(s).
- Specific activities done online.
- Required student work, such as assessments.

Take advantage of hypertext in the online schedule: link directly to the content, activities, or assessments as they occur (Figures 9.2, 9.4, and 9.6).

The schedule provides detail of the blended course as a whole, but can be summarized in a walkthrough of a typical lesson.

Overview of a Typical Lesson

Because each blended course experience may be different, providing an overview or walkthrough of a typical lesson within the syllabus helps students anticipate the regular workflow and expectations.

A lesson overview should:

- Explain how onsite and online activities are related.
- Describe what students will do each week or lesson.
- Explain how one lesson relates to other lessons.

Here is an example of a lesson overview from the syllabus of a blended Web design course.

How This Course Works: One Week = One Lesson
In this blended course, each lesson runs a full week, starting each Tuesday and ending the following Monday at 11:59 p.m.

We meet face to face each Thursday. During those meetings, we will discuss difficult lesson topics and work through your individual project challenges. I will not lecture, but will guide each of you to be an active participant in each meeting.

The rest of the course activities happen online, either collaboratively or on your own. The course website details these activities in lessons. Each lesson requires:

- **Readings and videos interspersed with brief self-assessment activities.** Study these materials before we meet each Thursday.
- **A quiz** that reviews material from the lesson and allows multiple attempts. Complete each quiz online before we meet on Thursday.
- **A project** that allows you to apply the knowledge you've gained in the lesson through authentic practice. Begin each project before we meet on Thursday. Submit each project to the online discussion forum by midnight on Monday.

- **A project discussion forum** where you will: (1) share your project; and (2) encourage and provide feedback on your colleague's projects. Participate in discussions throughout the week.

Completion of quizzes and participation in project discussions before we meet each week is imperative. I will base the face-to-face meetings on the sticking points and challenges I see in each.

The course is capped off with a comprehensive **final exam and a summative final project**.

An overview can simply be text, as in this example, but may also be done as a video screencast (see Chapter 7) that actually shows how students navigate through the course website, and explains how and when onsite activities are interwoven.

Description of Regular Activities and Assessments

As an extension of the overview of a typical lesson, a blended course syllabus provides a description of each regular activity and assessment by type (e.g., "Online Discussions" or "Self-Check Quizzes"). These descriptions let you explain what students should *generally* expect both online and onsite (save the detailed descriptions for the specific activity and assessment pages or tools in the LMS). They should include when, where, and how graded assignments should be submitted—online or onsite.

These descriptions should also explain how something that's done onsite connects to activities done online—and vice versa.

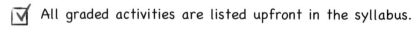 All graded activities are listed upfront in the syllabus.

☑ The manner of submission for graded assignments is clear.

Your Expectations for Student Participation

Clearly articulate your expectations for student participation — whether interacting with materials on the website, communicating with group members, or contributing to onsite class activities or discussions. This is critical because **blended courses require students to be more autonomous** and to take more control of the learning experience on their own time. Students need to be prepared to develop habits that contribute to their success week after week, in the looser rhythm of a blended course.

Explain to students that a blended course should constitute the same amount of work as a face-to-face or an online course. Also, be as explicit as possible in describing how much time students should expect to spend on each type of activity in each lesson. You can describe the time expectations in your lesson overview in the syllabus, as well as on the lesson introduction page.

Time Expectations

Students should plan to spend 9–12 hours a week in this course. This will vary from week to week, but a typical week may include:

- Orientation to the lesson (online): < 1hour.
- Reading (online, text): 2–3 hours.
- Watching online lectures and presentations (online): < 2 hours.
- Study and take reading quiz (online): < 1 hour.
- Onsite activities (face to face): 1 hour.
- Complete lab work or assignment (online, onsite): 2–3 hours.

Student Expectations for the Teacher

You may also want to include a brief description of what students can expect from the teacher in terms of communication methods, typical response time, amount of feedback, etc. This helps students understand that not only will you be responsive, but also that you have limitations on what you can do as a single teacher serving many students.

Syllabus communicates student expectations for participation.

 Students know when and how they will receive feedback from teachers.

Grading Schemes

Your expectations for students are described by the goals and outcomes for the course and its lessons, and by a general statement that you may provide in the syllabus. But your expectations are also set by the grading scheme that represents student performance during the course. A grading scheme may be a percentage, a scaled numeric score, or a letter grade.

Percentages are the most common basis for a grading scheme, and many teachers use weighted categories to calculate the final percentage (Table 9.1).

Table 9.1 Weighted categories should reflect the most important assessment activities, and constitute 100 percent of a final score

Category	Percentage
Participation	15%
Quizzes	15%
Projects	40%
Exams	30%
Total	**100%**

Weighting categories to constitute a final grade is more art than science, but it should reflect the course goals and outcomes. Remember, course goals and outcomes describe what the learner knows and does at the end of the course, so put emphasis on the assessments that provide the best evidence of student achievement.

In a blended course, you may find it easier to assess things that you couldn't measure in a face-to-face course. For example, class participation in a blended course may take place both onsite and online. Online participation is recorded by the course website, and can be quantified in terms of quantity and quality. This may allow you to more confidently put more weight on something such as class participation if it's an important part of student performance.

Other elements, such as quizzes, may be lower stakes in a blended course if you transform them into online, formative self-assessments as described in Chapters 6 and 7. A lower weight for such quizzes is appropriate if you have less confidence that quiz results reflect their individual learning. But such activities can still serve an important purpose as milestones and practice opportunities.

Online gradebooks support both teaching and learning: teachers can easily record student performance on assessments and activities; students can track their own progress on demand. Chapter 6 explains how an online gradebook works in a blended course.

☑ Grading criteria are outlined in the course syllabus and within the assignment or activity itself.

☑ The relationship between graded elements and the final grade is clear.

9.5　Summary and Standards

A blended course relies upon an online environment that is both thorough and easy to use. The course home page should serve as a hub, helping students immediately dive into relevant lesson activities. Lessons should clearly direct students down the path of learning—both online and onsite. Hyperlinks should be used wisely, making navigation to and from important activities easier without distracting students with non-critical content.

Keeping students focused on learning tasks is supported by the usability of the design. Teachers should focus on the student's experience when designing and sequencing activities in the course site, and should test usability by requesting feedback from others.

The final piece of this backward design model for blended courses is the construction of the syllabus. A blended course syllabus goes beyond basic course information to include a detailed, hyperlinked schedule, an overview or walkthrough of a typical lesson, activity descriptions, student expectations, and a grading scheme weighted appropriately for the redesigned blended course assessments.

- ☐ Lessons are introduced with stories, case studies, questions, or challenges to engage students' attention and make outcomes meaningful.

- ☐ Introductions and summaries are provided at the beginning and end of units.

- ☐ Instructions and requirements are stated simply, clearly, and logically.

- ☐ The writing style is clear, concise, and direct.

- ☐ Numbers are used to identify sequential steps in a task or process.

- ☐ Materials consistently indicate when activities or assessments take place onsite versus online.

- ☐ Online activities reference and connect with onsite activities, and vice versa.

- ☐ Direct links are provided to course materials and resources.

- ☐ Content elements are presented in a logical sequence.

- ☐ The course website is organized to guide and direct students toward course goals.

- ☐ The course website provides the shortest route for student navigation to relevant activities.

☐ The course website has been tested by non-experts to help identify any major usability problems.

☐ A syllabus including contact information, an outline, requirements, and guidelines is accessible from the start of the course throughout.

☐ Syllabus orients students to class workflow by providing a descriptive overview or walkthrough of a typical lesson.

☐ Contact information to advisers and technical help is provided in the syllabus.

☐ All graded activities are listed upfront in the syllabus.

☐ The manner of submission for graded assignments is clear.

☐ Syllabus communicates student expectations for participation.

☐ Students know when and how they will receive feedback from teachers.

☐ Grading criteria are outlined in the course syllabus and within the assignment or activity itself.

☐ The relationship between graded elements and the final grade is clear.

References and Further Reading

Amaral, K. E., & Shank, J. D. (2010). Enhancing student learning and retention with blended learning class guides. *Educause Quarterly*, 33(4), n4.

Aycock, A., Garnham, C., & Kaleta, R. (2002). Lessons learned from the hybrid course project. *Teaching with Technology Today*, 8(6).

Gerbic, P. (2009). Including online discussions within campus-based students' learning environments. In E. Stacey & P. Gerbic (Eds.), *Effective blended learning practices: Evidence-based perspectives in ICT-facilitated education* (pp. 21–38). Hershey, NH: Information Science Reference.

Grigorovici, D., Nam, S., & Russill, C. (2003). The effects of online syllabus interactivity on students' perception of the course and instructor. *Internet and higher education*, 6(1), 41–52.

Krug, S. (2006). *Don't make me think! A common sense approach to web usability* (2nd Ed.). Upper Saddle River, NJ: New Riders.

McGee, P., & Reis, A. (2012). Blended course design: A synthesis of best practices. *Journal of Asynchronous Learning Networks*, 16(4), 7–22.

Niederhauser, D., Reynolds, R., Salmen, D., & Skolmoski, P. (2000). The influence of cognitive load on learning from hypertext. *Journal of Educational Computing Research*, 23(3), 237–255.

Ross, B., & Gage, K. (2006). Global Perspectives on Blended Learning. *The handbook of blended learning: Global perspectives, local designs*, 155.

Chapter 10 Ongoing Improvements of the Blended Course

> What we call the beginning is often the end
> And to make an end is to make a beginning.
> The end is where we start from ...
>
> T. S. Eliot, *Four Quartets*, V

10.1 Making Improvement Part of the Process

As with every phase of this blended course design, teachers should start small, keep it simple, and use technologies that are familiar to teacher and students alike. This will result in a working blend so you can begin teaching the course.

As you teach, you should commit to regularly improving your blended course from the beginning. This is important because with blended learning your selection of either onsite or online modes can impact students' ability to reach learning goals and outcomes. The aims of ongoing improvement include:

- **Revise learning activities and assessments** so student outcomes improve.
- **Simplify the website** for students so they spend less time on the mechanics of workflow and focus more on learning.
- **Simplify class management tasks** and assessments for the teacher so she can spend more time on meaningful interactions with students.

Ongoing improvement is a cycle based on three phases (Figure 10.1):

- **Engaging** students with the course design.
- **Evaluating** student success with the design and understanding why the design was or wasn't successful.
- **Designing** a new version or revision based on what you discover through evaluation.

This model reduces the pressure to get everything "right" the first time, and provides opportunities to better implement blended course design standards, which should positively affect learning. Careful, small revisions—based on the best available information on instructional effectiveness—give you the best chance of knowing what design changes positively affect learning outcomes.

This chapter describes how you can develop habits that support continual improvement of your blended course without having to completely overhaul the course every semester.

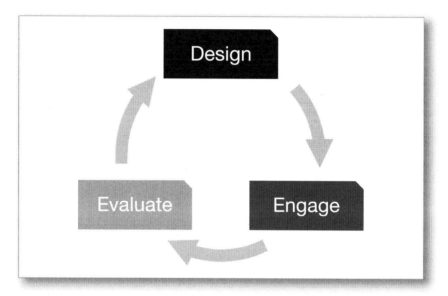

Figure 10.1 You can improve your blended course design by engaging students with the learning design, evaluating its effectiveness, and redesigning as necessary

 To Do

You now have a prototype of at least one lesson and a draft version of the syllabus for your blended course. Use the lesson prototype as a model for other lessons as you build the rest of your course. Plan to make revisions as you teach the course based on student performance.

10.2 Engaging Students through Teaching

The practice of teaching is a subject worthy of its own guide, but there are a number of tips we can share that will help you effectively engage students around your blended course design:

- **Anticipate problems with technology** and try to prepare for them. Have a "plan B" if something goes wrong. For example, if the Learning Management System (LMS) goes down, try an online discussion via email.
- **Avoid adding new activities or tools mid-stream.** If you have a great idea, save it for a future lesson or future semester.
- **Continually encourage students** by sharing your expectations and your vision of what they *will* accomplish and who they will become.
- Remind students that **technology should not be a barrier** to learning, and tell them they can go for help if they get stuck.
- Dedicate yourself to providing **swift and meaningful feedback**.
- **Give constructive feedback** by recognizing the positive things in a student's work before identifying things that need to be fixed or changed.
- **Learn to use the technology like a pro.** The more fluent you are with the tools, the smoother the course will run, and the easier it will be for you to focus on teaching.
- **Make your own journal entries each week** on how the course is going. Use these notes to inform future revisions based on what is and isn't working.

10.3 How Do You Know What is Working?

Some teachers will engage in formal and rigorous evaluation methods of their course design in order to determine its effectiveness. However, there are a number of indicators that are readily available to you, which can suggest the effectiveness of your blended course.

Student Performance

Teachers can look to course assessments to understand whether or not the class is performing adequately in the blended course. Student performance in a blended course can be compared with results from face-to-face or fully online courses—presuming that the outcomes are the same, and assessments are equivalent.

Analytics

Learning analytics are the data that describe student usage of the course website and their performance on activities and assessments. Some LMSs include visualizations of user analytics that can help you understand how students behave in the course, and lead you to constructive questions about course design.

For example Figure 10.2 is an analytics chart that shows the timeliness of activity submission for the entire class.

This chart shows that many students missed the first activity— Quiz 1. Many more students completed the second and third activities, but a significant proportion of students completed these late. This information doesn't say *why* this happened,

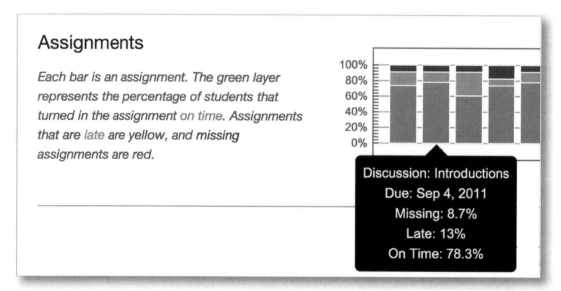

Assignments

Each bar is an assignment. The green layer represents the percentage of students that turned in the assignment on time. Assignments that are late are yellow, and missing assignments are red.

100%
80%
60%
40%
20%
0%

Discussion: Introductions
Due: Sep 4, 2011
Missing: 8.7%
Late: 13%
On Time: 78.3%

Figure 10.2 This bar graph shows timeliness of assignment submission for the class

Note

Most of the evaluation indicators described here do not conclusively prove the effectiveness of your instruction, but should be used in combination to paint a picture of the course, and help guide future iterations.

Learner Dashboards

Learning analytics seem especially valuable to teachers and administrators seeking to understand what their students are actually doing and how that might relate to different instructional strategies. But let's not forget the students themselves. Students who have access to their own analytics (e.g., through an online dashboard) might self-monitor their progress and use the reports to adjust their time on task and performance.

And why shouldn't we deliver learning analytics with the students? Isn't it, after all, *their* data?

but it could prompt you to ask questions, such as: Are students not aware of what is required of them early in the course? Does the course website design obstruct students from completing these activities?

Different analytics tools provide different visualizations. Some common visualizations include:

- Student activity in the course website over time.
- Page visits and time spent on pages.
- Difficulty of quiz or exam questions.
- Timeliness of assignment submissions (Figure 10.2).
- Student attainment of course outcomes.
- Class performance (ranges, averages) on activities and assessments (Figure 10.3).

While most learning analytics aim to *predict* student performance in order to help teachers intervene, they may also reflect gaps in instruction where students are shown to not be interacting or succeeding at desired levels.

 We share more information on analytics, including links to valuable resources, on our website.

Student Feedback

Student journals can be used regularly in the course to ask students to reflect upon their learning, identify difficult parts of a lesson, and develop plans for success in future lessons.

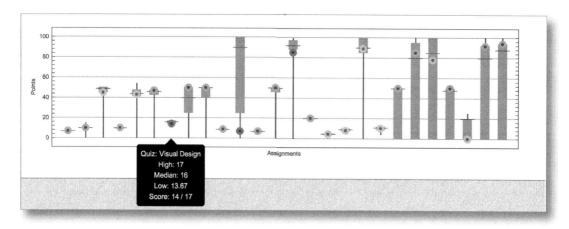

Figure 10.3 This analytics visualization shows the range of students scores on different assignments as a box plot, with the current student's score in that range identified by the circles

While student journals serve as a useful learning activity, they can also inform teachers as to the difficulty and effectiveness of the course.

The course evaluations is a standard administrative tool used to collect general feedback from students on their perception of the course at the end of the term or semester. Institutional course evaluations may not provide specific feedback about *blended* course design, but can often highlight general strengths or weaknesses that stand out to students.

Student surveys can be created online by the teacher. Questions should be tailored to the blended course design. You may include the survey several times throughout the course the first time you teach it, since you'll want to make changes to future lessons if something is not working.

When you are more confident in the design of your blended course, student surveys may be used just twice during the course (e.g. at midterm and at the end of the course).

Some very simple and very useful survey questions include:

- Which online and onsite activities or resources are working well for you in this course?
- What might be done to increase or improve your learning in this course?

Tip
Free online survey tools include Google Forms (docs. google.com) or SurveyMonkey (surveymonkey. com).

Likert scale questions can also provide insight into students' perception of the course and their learning. These ask for agreement and disagreement (e.g., five-point scale with strongly agree on one side, strongly disagree on the other) with statements such as those shown in Table 10.1.

The statements in Table 10.1 are carefully worded to not guide students to the answer that the teacher wants to hear. They do touch on student opinion of blended courses and the value they place on online and onsite activities. They also ask about the design of the blended course in some major areas, such as clarity of instructions, ease of use of the website, and the workload that the course requires. Several of the questions are learning-centric.

Table 10.1 A student survey for a blended course

Opinion	Strongly Agree	Agree	No	Disagree	Strongly Disagree
I was glad to find out this course was blended					
Onsite (face-to-face) time helps me learn					
Online activities are more engaging than onsite activities					
I don't really need to come to the face-to-face class					
Instructions for online activities are confusing					
Most people will easily figure out how to use the course website					
I'm learning a lot in this course					
I don't worry about the technology getting in the way when I'm working online					
This feels like more work than a regular face-to-face course					

Student feedback is just one source of information on how well your blended course design is working. It may not show the true effectiveness of your teaching, but it can identify significant problems with course design or real possibilities for improvement.

Note that student feedback is *not* meant to simply measure "customer satisfaction"; rather, you should ask students to reflect on the effectiveness of the learning experience in order to make it better for themselves and future students. Blended courses should pay special attention to questions that distinguish between the relative value of conducting activities online or onsite. You'll likely find that students are keenly aware of what works online versus face to face.

Students who feel that their input matters may be more engaged and motivated to persist—an important factor in engaging their hearts and leading you to affective outcomes.

☑ A variety of information (student performance data, feedback, etc.) is used to evaluate the effectiveness of course design.

☑ Evaluation of the course design is applied as revisions in future iterations.

10.4 Revising Blended Course Design

We've identified phases whereby you can continually improve a blended course by iterating through using, evaluating, and revising the design. Even if you're redesigning a single lesson or the entire course, you can rely on the backward design model to focus on the effectiveness of each element.

Improving teaching and learning in a blended course can be challenging because there are so many variables to consider, from tools and technology used, to the design of activities, to individual students' background knowledge and attitudes. To ensure the success of a blended course, you should always

Reflection

As you reflect on your course design, focus on the standards provided throughout this book. The standards checklist in Appendix 1 is a compilation of all standards in an easy-to-use form (you'll find an online and printer-ready version on the website). Check the standards that you've hit. Highlight or star any standards that you want to focus on in future iterations. Share the standards list with colleagues and discuss how well they apply to blended course design.

question whether or not the activities and assessments are better suited for online or onsite, and if outcomes would be affected by switching modes.

Beware of the risk to students if every learning experience is essentially a radical experiment that could fail. Instead, **make small changes over time**. Monitor the impact of those changes using methods and tools described above.

It's easier to do revisions right after teaching a lesson than after the semester is over. Apply feedback and the results of assessments to your lesson designs while they are still fresh in your mind. This also creates an opportunity to apply revisions to subsequent lessons as needed.

Another way to engage in continual improvement is through seeking out colleagues in your institution that are also teaching blended courses. See if there are organized professional development workshops that focus on teaching with technology. If not, consider organizing local meet-ups with other teachers who are interested in sharing and learning from each other. Teachers who are more experienced with blended teaching and course design can peer-mentor other teachers. Learning from others is a great way to gain perspective, discover new approaches, and stay engaged in the practice of blended teaching and learning.

 We've shared a list of websites and journals that include more ideas and research for blended teaching and learning.

Plan to improve your course design in small ways, whenever you touch the course.

10.5   Teaching as Sharing

Teaching is sharing; without sharing there is no education.

David Wiley (2010)

You can share your own experiences of teaching a blended course beyond your local community by publishing on the open Web. This provides an opportunity for others to benefit from your ideas and insights, as well as for you to gain feedback from a global community of teachers. Here are some ideas:

- **Blogging.** Your blended teaching journal can be published as a blog (just be sure to omit student information).
- **Publishing.** More formal evaluation or research on blended teaching can be submitted to academic journals.
- **Sharing.** Your own blended course materials and activities can be shared as **open educational resources** so that other teachers can reuse and build upon your work.

WEB The website lists academic journals and publications relevant to blended learning that you may want to read or even submit your own work to.

WEB See the website for a list of open educational resource projects where you can find and share teaching and learning materials.

When teachers share what they know openly and freely with their students, the intent is to help students change their lives for the better. Internet technology enables us to share differently and more efficiently within the classroom and beyond. Blended learning requires that we begin moving the metaphorical walls of the classroom to encompass online spaces. This creates a powerful potential for teachers to connect formal, classroom learning to informal learning in the real world using online tools and resources—the kind of learning that students will have to do—indeed, already do—in their own lives, on a daily basis. We can let learning permeate the bounds of the classroom in small ways (e.g. by simply sharing our own teaching practices, or even just encouraging students to share what they've learned on the open Web).

WEB **See the website for a list of blogging platforms that you can start using today in order to share your blended teaching practices.**

10.6 Summary and Standards

Teachers who plan to improve their blended course design from the beginning will be more likely to help students succeed in reaching learning goals by using the best blend of online and onsite modes. The aims of your revisions should include improving outcomes by revising assessments and activities, and simplifying both the website and activities to reduce non-essential work for both teacher and students.

Teachers can also increase success by committing to engage with students during the course in meaningful ways. Technology can make it easier for teachers to evaluate the effectiveness of their course through analytics, surveys, etc. This information—along with community interactions—can be used to revise the blended course, one lesson at a time.

Technology not only enables new blended teaching and learning practices, but it also enables sharing of those practices and experiences on the open Web. Engaging students in the spaces where they live, using the tools that they are familiar with, will help students transfer learning—both formal and informal—to their daily lives.

☐ A variety of information (student performance data, feedback, etc.) is used to evaluate the effectiveness of course design.

☐ Evaluation of the course design is applied as revisions in future iterations.

☐ Plan to improve your course design in small ways, whenever you touch the course.

References and Further Reading

Evans, J. R., & Mathur, A. (2005). The value of online surveys. *Internet Research*, 15(2), 195–219.

Hensley, G. (2005). Creating a hybrid college course: Instructional design notes and recommendations for beginners. *Journal of Online Learning and Teaching*, 1(2), 1–7.

Siemens, G., & Long, P. (2011). Penetrating the fog: Analytics in learning and education. *Educause Review*, 46(5), 30–32.

Wiley, D. (2010, March). *Openness and the future of education.* Presentation at TEDxNYED, New York. Retrieved from http://youtube.com/watch?v=Rb0syrgsH6M.

Blended Course Standards Checklist

Course Goals and Learning Outcomes

☐ A concise course description identifies the learner audience, course goals, and instructional strategy (Chapter 5).

☐ Course goals are clearly written and broadly describe the successful learner at the end of the course (Chapter 5).

☐ Learning outcomes for a blended course are identical to those of the onsite version (Chapters 1, 5).

☐ Learning outcomes are measurable and specific (Chapter 5).

☐ Learning outcomes relate to goals and are learner-focused (Chapter 5).

☐ Sufficient time is allotted for attainment of each learning outcome (Chapter 5).

☐ Resources and activities support learning outcomes (Chapters 4, 7).

☐ Online or onsite modes are chosen by how their qualities best support learning activities and outcomes (Chapter 4).

☐ The relationship between learning outcomes and assessments is evident (Chapters 6, 9).

Ease of Communication

☐ The writing style is clear, concise, and direct (Chapter 9).

☐ Instructions and requirements are stated simply, clearly, and logically (Chapters 6, 9).

☐ Contact information to advisers and technical help is provided in the syllabus (Chapter 9).

☐ Syllabus communicates student expectations for participation (Chapter 9).

☐ Syllabus orients students to class workflow by providing a descriptive overview or walkthrough of a typical lesson (Chapter 9).

☐ Students are given clear expectations and criteria for assignments. Examples are included for clarification when needed (Chapter 6).

☐ The manner of submission for graded assignments is clear (Chapters 6, 9).

☐ Criteria and procedures for peer review and evaluation are clear (Chapter 6).

☐ Materials consistently indicate when activities or assessments take place onsite versus online (Chapter 9).

☐ Numbers are used to identify sequential steps in a task or process (Chapter 9).

Pedagogical and Organizational Design

☐ A syllabus including contact information, an outline, requirements, and guidelines is accessible from the start of the course throughout (Chapter 9).

☐ Introductions and summaries are provided at the beginning and end of units (Chapter 9).

☐ Blocks of information are broken up into incremental chunks to support memory (Chapter 7).

☐ Content elements are presented in a logical sequence (Chapter 9).

- [ ] Pedagogical steps build progressively, one upon the other, as is appropriate to the subject matter (Chapter 7).

- [ ] New information, including teacher feedback, is followed by opportunities for students to apply the information (Chapters 6, 7).

- [ ] Online activities reference and connect with onsite activities, and vice versa (Chapters 7, 8, 9).

- [ ] A blended course is the same amount of work as online or onsite versions (Chapter 4).

Engaged Learning

- [ ] Activities are frequent and varied (Chapter 7).

- [ ] Activities encourage interactions that involve course content and personal communication (Chapter 7).

- [ ] Lessons are introduced with stories, case studies, questions, or challenges to engage students' attention and make outcomes meaningful (Chapter 9).

- [ ] Stories, anecdotes, emotion, or human conflict are used to engage learners and show real-world relevance when appropriate.

- [ ] Presentations are designed to engage and support learner attention.

- [ ] Presentations include examples, models, case studies, illustrations, etc. for clarification (Chapter 7).

- [ ] Reflection and reflective activities come up throughout the course (Chapter 8).

- [ ] Materials are authentic or relate to real-life applications (Chapter 7).

- [ ] Content is designed to be simple and clear so as to avoid information overload (e.g. avoid narrating while written text is visible, using distracting images for decoration, presenting too much information at once, etc.) (Chapter 7).

Collaboration and Community

☐ Activities encourage active interactions that involve course content and personal communication (Chapter 8).

☐ Learners are encouraged to interact with others (classmates, course guests, etc.) to benefit from their expertise (Chapter 8).

☐ Learners take responsibility for their learning and, at times, the learning of others (Chapter 8).

☐ An online space (e.g. discussion board, social network) is in place for students to meet outside the class (Chapter 8).

☐ When blogs are used, they are established as learner-owned spaces for sharing and discussion (Chapter 8).

☐ Students are encouraged to share resources as is appropriate (Chapter 8).

☐ Discussions are designed to capitalize on the asynchronous nature of online and the synchronous nature of onsite (Chapter 8).

☐ Activities allow students to retain their privacy on their own terms (Chapter 8).

Assessments and Feedback

☐ Course includes ongoing and frequent assessment (Chapter 6).

☐ Graded elements are clearly distinguished from those that are ungraded (Chapter 6).

☐ Graded assignments are varied (e.g. special projects, reflective assignments, research papers, case studies, presentations, group work, etc.) (Chapter 6).

☐ Assessments determine the degree to which learners have achieved the required learning outcomes (Chapters 4, 6).

☐ Onsite assessments capitalize on physical presence, immediacy, and human interaction (Chapter 6).

☐ Criteria/rubrics clearly inform learners as to how they will be assessed on specific assignments and provide useful feedback (Chapters 6, 8).

☐ Self-correcting and self-assessment activities are used throughout the course to support practice and increase flexibility of pacing (Chapters 6, 7).

☐ Feedback from a variety of sources corrects, clarifies, amplifies, and extends learning (Chapter 6).

☐ Automated feedback provides clarification on incorrect answers and elaborates on correct answers (Chapter 6).

☐ Teacher feedback is provided in a timely fashion (Chapter 6).

☐ Students know when and how they will receive feedback from teachers (Chapters 6, 9).

Grading

☐ The size of and due date for graded assignments is reasonable (Chapter 6).

☐ The consequences of plagiarism, cheating, and failure to properly cite copyrighted materials are emphasized (Chapter 6).

☐ All graded activities are listed upfront in the syllabus (Chapter 9).

☐ Grading criteria are outlined in the course syllabus and within the assignment or activity itself (Chapter 9).

☐ The relationship between graded elements and the final grade is clear (Chapter 6).

☐ Students can easily track their progress (Chapter 6).

Ease of Access

☐ The course website is organized to guide and direct students toward course goals (Chapter 9).

☐ The course website provides the shortest route for student navigation to relevant activities (Chapter 9).

☐ Direct links are provided to course materials and resources (Chapter 9).

☐ Audio and video material appearing within a lesson should be brief (Chapter 7).

☐ Resource material is accessible to all students in commonly used formats (Chapter 7).

☐ Non-essential materials that may present extraneous cognitive load are avoided (Chapter 7).

Preparation and Revisions

☐ Plan to improve your course design in small ways, whenever you touch the course (Chapters 4, 5, 10).

☐ Evaluations of the course design are applied as revisions in future iterations (Chapters 4, 10).

☐ A variety of information (student performance data, feedback, etc.) is used to evaluate the effectiveness of course design (Chapter 10).

☐ The course website has been tested by non-experts to identify any major usability problems (Chapter 9).

Key Cognitive Processes in Bloom's Taxonomy

Matching Outcomes to Categories of the Cognitive Domain

You've probably been exposed to Bloom's Taxonomy of the cognitive domain in the past, and it's easy to take it for granted. We reintroduce it here because the taxonomy is a useful tool for planning learning outcomes and, subsequently, assessments and activities.

As you write your specific learning outcomes, identify which level of the cognitive domain each falls into. Be sure that learners have the prerequisite cognitive skills to achieve the learning outcome. If they don't, you may need to plan activities into the unit that remediate or otherwise address these foundational skills.

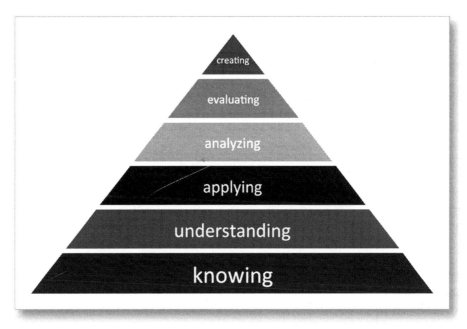

Figure A2.1 This layered pyramid represents a progression of cognitive skills for each level of Bloom's (revised) Taxonomy

Bloom's Taxonomy applies to the *cognitive* domain (i.e. the broad area of mental knowledge and skills). Psychologists have identified other domains, such as psychomotor (i.e. physical skill) and affective (e.g. emotions, attitudes, etc.).

These other domains play a critical role in learner success and should not be neglected. While this book focuses on designing assessments and activities, primarily for the cognitive domain, it also encourages attention toward the affective domain by means of encouraging student self-regulation for success.

As you write learning outcomes, make a note of which levels of the cognitive domain will be assessed. For example:

- Name the plates and boundaries that make up the surface of the earth's crust [know].
- Sketch and describe the interior layers of the earth [understand].
- Describe the theory of "continental drift" [understand].
- Analyze evidence of seafloor spreading, including hot spots [analyze, apply].
- Apply the theory of seafloor spreading to explain different seafloor sediment thicknesses and ages [apply, understand].

If you find it difficult to determine which levels of the cognitive domain your outcomes fall into, see Table A2.1, which associates each level with helpful verbs.

Not all courses will deal in every level of the cognitive domain. It's not unusual for foundational courses, such as a first-year biology course, to only engage the first two or three levels. And some advanced courses may attend to only the higher levels of the cognitive domain, engaging the lower levels only incidentally. Conversely, some teachers may find that the lower levels of the cognitive domain can be addressed as a natural outcome of *doing* at the higher levels.

Each category or level of Bloom's Taxonomy of the cognitive domain can be elaborated into a number of key processes. These process verbs are useful as you write specific learning outcomes.

Table A2.1 Cognitive domains and associated verbs

Cognitive Domain	Key Processes
Know	Recognize
	Recall
Understand	Interpret
	Classify/group
	Exemplify
	Infer
	Compare
	Explain
	Summarize
Apply	Execute
	Implement
Analyze	Differentiate/distinguish
	Organize/structure
	Attribute/represent
Evaluate	Check/verify
	Critique
Create	Plan/design
	Generate or hypothesize
	Produce or construct

The Center for Excellence in Learning and Teaching provides an interactive 3D model of Bloom's Taxonomy of the cognitive domain with a four-level **knowledge dimension** on its website (www.celt.iastate.edu/teaching/RevisedBlooms1.html).

References

Heer, R. (2011). A model of learning objectives – Based on A taxonomy for learning, teaching, and assessing: A revision of Bloom's taxonomy of educational objectives. Ohio State University, Retrieved January 2012, http://www.celt.iastate.edu/teaching/RevisedBlooms1.html

Krathwohl, D. R. (2002). A revision of Bloom's taxonomy: An overview. *Theory into Practice*, 41(4), 212–218.

Index